Clifton Park - Halfmoon Public Library
475 Moe Road
Clifton Park, New York 12065

W9-ATG-773

READING IS FUNNY!

Motivating Kids to Read with Riddles

Dee Anderson

American Library Association

Chicago   2009

Dee Anderson, who earned her MLS from the University of Iowa, has worked in public and school libraries since high school and has enjoyed reading and riddles for as long as she can remember. Teacher requests prompted her to start a riddle file years ago. Anderson has implemented activities in this book with children in libraries, after-school programs, and enrichment classes for the gifted. She has also presented at workshops and conferences for teachers and parents. She wrote *Amazingly Easy Puppet Plays* (American Library Association, 1997) and provided children's activities for four publications of the Colonel Davenport Historical Foundation. Since 2000 a local newspaper has run her monthly column on children's books and reading. Anderson currently works at the Rock Island Primary Academy in Rock Island, Illinois.

While extensive effort has gone into ensuring the reliability of information appearing in this book, the publisher makes no warranty, express or implied, on the accuracy or reliability of the information, and does not assume and hereby disclaims any liability to any person for any loss or damage caused by errors or omissions in this publication.

The paper used in this publication meets the minimum requirements of American National Standard for Information Sciences—Permanence of Paper for Printed Library Materials, ANSI Z39.48-1992. ∞

Library of Congress Cataloging-in-Publication Data
Anderson, Dee.
  Reading is funny! : motivating kids to read with riddles / Dee Anderson.
        p. cm.
  Includes bibliographical references and index.
  ISBN-13: 978-0-8389-0957-7 (alk. paper)
1. School libraries—Activity programs—United States. 2. Riddles, Juvenile. 3. Humor in education.
4. Reading promotion—United States. I. Title.
Z675.S3A53 2009
027.80973—dc22   2008000980

Copyright © 2009 by the American Library Association. All rights reserved except those which may be granted by Sections 107 and 108 of the Copyright Revision Act of 1976.

ISBN-13: 978-0-8389-0957-7

Printed in the United States of America
13 12 11 10 09   5 4 3 2 1

For Karen A. and Emily Young,
who inspired this riddle:

Why are good friends like lobsters?

They come through in a "pinch."

Thanks for coming through in a pinch.
Your assistance was invaluable.

And for my family,

Richard L. and Jewel H. Anderson
and Susan L. Granet.

Thanks for giving me a sense
of humor in the first place.

Without that, this book
wouldn't exist.

Contents

14   Fun(ny) and Games: Riddles about Sports   **143**

**15   Talking Turnips: Riddles for Talking Turnip Bulletin Boards,
Games, and Story**   **149**

Appendix C is also available on the book's website:
www.ala.org/editions/extras/Anderson09577.

Acknowledgments

What did the army general say when the Pentagon gave him new armored vehicles?

"'Tanks.'"

Special "tanks" to Jewel H. Anderson (aka Mom) for instilling in me a love of reading; to all the teachers who taught me how to read and write; to the staffs of the Moline (Illinois) Public Library and the Rock Island (Illinois) Public Library for helping me obtain the many books I previewed for the bibliography; and to the staff of ALA Editions.

The following people have encouraged my endeavors, provided much-needed technical support, or shared riddles, ideas, or information adapted for this book. I've appreciated the way they've made my life richer: Joan Allee, Caroline Feller Bauer, Mary Bowker, Mike Breidenstein, Lisa Broadbent, Brenda Carmen, Jeremy Conaway, Ann Cottay, Janet DeDecker, Debra J. Depaepe, Laura Hall, Angela Hunt, Janet Olson Johnson, Josh Johnson, Eloise L. Kinney, Mary Kmoch, Bonnie Lawhorn, Kris Gayman Leinicke, Mike MacKenna, Tera McCormick-Skinner, Laura Pelehach, Dee Robbins, Marcus Robinson, Sheila Sheer, Theresa Shores, Sue Spurgetis, Ellen M. Stahl, Malia Sullivan, Alice Traylor, Megan Trinrud, Mabe Wassell, Jan Welch, Danielle Wild, Kathy Woodward, Emily Young, and Karen A. Young.

I'd also like to "tank" everyone who has shared riddles with me over the years or laughed at ones I've told. I'm also grateful to the authors of all the riddle books I've read.

Introduction

Why do skeletons read riddle books?
to tickle their funny bones

EIGHT REASONS TO SHARE RIDDLES WITH CHILDREN

Why should librarians, teachers, and other adults who work with children share riddles with them? There are eight great reasons to share riddles with children.

1. To Tickle Their Funny Bones

The ability to laugh brightens our days and helps us keep going, because laughter almost immediately relaxes the brain, relieves stress, and releases endorphins that make us feel good. Recently, a crying child cheered up when I read him riddles. When the teacher in charge of our school's malfunctioning photocopiers sent everyone an e-mail about their proper use, I replied with riddles about Xerox machines. Immediately she responded: "Thanks. I needed some comic relief."

Because a sense of humor makes life more bearable, shouldn't we help the children in our lives develop this valuable coping skill?

2. To Tickle Their Brains

Riddles aren't just good for laughs, however. They provide excellent mental exercise as well. By the age of six or seven, children have developed what Swiss psychologist Jean Piaget called "concrete operational thinking." Because playing with different meanings of words is fun, riddles motivate kids to work out their new intellectual skill.

Riddles are a wonderful (and fun) way for children to understand that words can have more than one meaning. I think it teaches them to be more flexible with the language and to try and think about those multiple-meaning words in a different context. Riddles are also a good

1

way to teach inference, using clues to determine a specific answer. (Malia Sullivan, speech language therapist)

Riddles increase background knowledge, enhance deductive and inductive thinking skills, and improve visual imaging needed for better reading skills. Most importantly, short readings for short attention spans tickle the brain's development and galvanize a *love* of reading. (Dee Robbins, reading teacher)

3. To Expand Their Vocabularies

Children might not know all the words in riddles, but they'll want to learn them to get the jokes. Looking up unfamiliar words in a dictionary or hearing definitions from adults helps kids develop the vocabulary necessary for reading comprehension. Children can't possibly understand what they read or hear if they don't know what the words mean. (Just think how much trouble you have making sense out of anything loaded with medical terms or technical jargon.) Riddles help children increase their background knowledge as well, which also fosters comprehension.

4. To Help Them Learn to Read

We all do more of what gives us pleasure. A college instructor enjoyed Bennett Cerf's *Riddle-De-Dee* so much when she was a child that unfamiliar concepts and vocabulary didn't faze her. She simply asked her grandmother about them, thereby learning to read in the process. A Title I teacher reported with pleasure that one of her reluctant students read more after discovering the joy of riddle books. A mother wrote *Family Fun* magazine that she once tucked notes into her son's lunch to encourage him to read. When he threw her missives away without even a glance, she started slipping riddles in with his sandwiches. This worked! Because her son enjoyed the riddles, he reread them to classmates throughout the day. Rereading the same material repeatedly helps children improve their fluency.

Timothy V. Rasinski, a reading expert who wrote *The Fluent Reader*, advocates that all reading must have a purpose. Savoring the pleasure of making others laugh certainly provides a purpose for reading. Score another point for riddles!

5. To Give Children a Sense of Mastery

The triumph of being one up on those not in the know provides another purpose for reading. Sharing riddles lets children have all the answers for a change. It allows them to fool other people—even grown-ups. Wow! What a heady switch from feeling that everyone else knows more than you do and from always being told what to do!

6. To Bond with Children

Sharing laughs helps people feel closer.

7. To Make Visiting the Library Fun

Reading and hearing riddles make trips to the library fun. Anticipating them before the actual visit can make children eager to walk through your doors.

8. To Improve Your Image and Their Perception of Reading

Showing your playful side helps dispel those "dragon lady" stereotypes that persist about librarians. Positive feelings about people who love reading might help foster good feelings about the act of reading itself. When children learn that the riddle they laughed at came from a book, they see that opening book covers opens up worlds of fun.

SIMPLE WAYS TO START SHARING RIDDLES

A few tips will help you and the children get more fun out of riddles. Some riddles work best when you share them in writing:

What prehistoric reptiles were black-and-blue?
"dino-sores"

Other riddles are more suitable for sharing orally:

If April showers bring May flowers, what do May flowers bring?
Pilgrims

Delivering punch lines with vocal expression and appropriate gestures enhances their humor. For example, say "pew" distastefully while holding your nose with one hand and waving your other hand in front of you when sharing the following riddle.

What did Christopher Robin call his pet skunk?
Winnie-the-"Pew"

Pretend to shiver during the punch line to this next riddle.

What do you call your Thanksgiving turkey when it's still in the freezer?
a "brrr-d"

Share Riddles while Checking Out Books

When I worked in a public library, I enjoyed sharing riddles while checking out patrons' books. If you decide to try this, learn one to three riddles each week. Consider choosing riddles that fit the time of year (see chapter 13), the sports season (see chapter 14), the weather (see chapter 16), or a current event (either in your library, your community, or the world).

A slight change of wording makes riddles fit new situations. For example, I adapted a sports riddle to fit the state speech tournament when it took place in our city.

Why did Cinderella's team lose the speech tournament?

They had a pumpkin for a coach.

(The original was "Why was Cinderella such a lousy baseball player?

She had a pumpkin for a coach.")

If this seems like too much bother, share any riddles that tickle your funny bone.

Unlike Trix cereal, riddles aren't just for kids. Some grown-ups enjoy them, too. One night a father who usually brought his children to the library came in alone. As he checked out, he remarked sheepishly, "When I was here with the kids last week, you asked them some riddles. Do you know any tonight?" While working on *Reading Is Funny!* one afternoon, I tried out scouting riddles on our school's Cub Scout leader. After that he seemed to expect a riddle every week.

Riddle of the Week

Post a new riddle at the circulation desk each week. To show children that opening books opens up worlds of fun, write "For more fun, read our riddle books" at the bottom of the page. If you copied the riddle from a book, put its title under the answer. (To teach library skills, see "Riddle of the Week" in chapter 3.)

Share Riddles through Your Website

Put a riddle or two on your home page so people will see them as soon as they visit your site. Change riddles weekly or monthly.

Fill In Odd Moments of Waiting Time with Riddles

Will the dismissal bell ring in just a few minutes? Are you stuck in line because the class that takes PE ahead of yours is running late? Ask a riddle or two.

Introduce Books with Riddles

Before or after reading a story aloud, share a related riddle. Incorporate riddles into booktalks. (See chapter 8 for titles that probably appear in many collections.)

For other literature, find riddles that match their subjects. When matching riddles to books, brainstorm as many related subjects as possible. For example, either cat riddles from chapter 10 or witch riddles from chapter 12 might work with Caralyn Buehner and Mark Buehner's *A Job for Wittilda* (Dial, 1993). Pizza riddles might apply, too, if you know any.

Change wording to make riddles fit books. Don't ask, "Why did the dog . . . ?" Ask instead, "Why did Martha [or Shiloh or Sounder] . . . ?" Substitute "Jack's giant" for "elephant" when answers involve being big, or use "the Littles" instead of "leprechauns" when answers involve being short.

If you can't find a riddle that covers a particular book, make one up! Chapter 6 provides tips to start you off.

Share Riddles during Daily Announcements at School

If you work in a school, ask the principal to let you share a riddle during daily announcements. If every day seems like too much, consider doing this once a week or only during special occasions like Children's Book Week, Dr. Seuss's birthday, and National Library Week. To involve students, see chapter 2.

Celebrate National Library Week, Children's Book Week, and Your Summer Reading Program

Hold drawings to give away books during special occasions. Children can enter by answering riddles. (See "Interactive Bulletin Boards" in chapter 1 and "Riddle of the Week" in chapter 3.)

NOTES ABOUT THIS BOOK AND HOW TO USE IT

To encourage you to incorporate riddles into your program as much as possible, I've organized *Reading Is Funny!* in a way that I hope you'll find easy to use. Material appears alphabetically by subject matter as much as possible; *see* and *see also* references throughout the text guide you to related contents.

Part 1 suggests ways to motivate kids to read with riddles. Each chapter offers a number of ideas for a given method, and some ideas can be presented using multiple methods. For example, "The Talking Turnip," a folktale reproduced in appendix A, and "The Loony Library," the imaginary collection of silly titles in chapter 9, work with bulletin boards in chapter 1 and games in chapter 3.

Chapter 1 describes how to create simple seasonal and year-round bulletin boards that promote reading. The interactive bulletin boards stimulate children to think critically by allowing them to match book jackets to riddles, pair questions with answers, figure out mystery words, or decode secret messages. The suggestions don't require artistic talent to implement, because they call for book jackets, pictures from old calendars and magazines, and cutouts. (See appendix C for patterns you can enlarge.)

Suggestions in chapter 2 give children a humorous way to practice reading for a purpose, public speaking, and writing with proper penmanship, spelling, capitalization, and punctuation. Children can read riddles during your school's daily announcements, illustrate riddles, make riddle books, and fill a jar with riddles. You can collect riddles from kids to share through bulletin boards, bookmarks, newspapers, newsletters, and websites.

Chapter 3 tells how to incorporate riddles into quiet and active games you can play anywhere. Most are noncompetitive.

"The Talking Turnip" and "The Loony Library" inspired card games that let children match questions to quotes or titles to authors. Play Talking Turnip and Loony Library like Old Maid. Riddle Roundup follows the rules of Concentration (aka Memory). To encourage children to work together, play these games' noncompetitive variations, Who Said That? and Who Wrote That?

Crack the Code! encourages children to practice alphabet skills while decoding answers to riddles. Get It Together lets children assemble puzzles to read riddles. (To play some of the quiet games with activity sheets, see appendix C.)

In Find Your Partner, children move around to find the player with the other half of their riddle. Egg Hunt is just what the name implies. In Pass It On, a noncompetitive variation of Hot Potato, children read riddles instead of dropping out. The Toll-Bridge Troll Game lets children act out a picture book by answering riddles to cross an imaginary bridge.

Riddle of the Week and the Loony Library Book Hunt teach children how to find books in your library.

Chapter 4 describes how to create PR handouts that use riddles to promote your library and suggests places to distribute them in your community. (See appendix C for samples.) It also provides ideas to attract families to your booth at community events. These include assembling puzzles, making puppets, and figuring out mystery words and coded messages.

Chapter 5 provides directions for making paper plate and paper bag puppets with children. Kids can use these creations to share the reproducible riddles provided in appendix C. Chapter 5 also tells how you can use puppets to ask riddles or present puppet skits. Novice puppeteers can learn how to make puppets out of mittens and socks plus get a few tips for giving them life. (See appendix A for three skits that include riddles.)

Because *Reading Is Funny!* can't provide riddles for every book and situation, chapter 6 offers tips for making up riddles. It also teaches how to keep a file to supply your future riddle needs.

Part 2 supplies hundreds of riddles that support the ideas in the first part. Each chapter covers a different subject (e.g., animals, holidays, and sports). Chapters with book-related riddles come first, with other chapters following in alphabetical order by their subject matter. (The last chapter, "Odds and Ends," includes riddles on popular subjects that don't fit anywhere else.) Each chapter subdivides topics alphabetically. *See* and *see also* references guide you to related riddles.

Although my name stands alone on the cover, I don't pretend to have made up every riddle in *Reading Is Funny!* Some *are* original. The rest are adaptations or rewrites of riddles in a file I've kept ever since patrons requested riddles on eggs and volcanoes in the early 1990s. Unfortunately, giving credit where it's due is impossible. Because I never anticipated writing a book when I started the file, I copied riddles I liked without citing sources.

Reading Is Funny! excludes riddles involving underwear, bodily functions, disrespectful attitudes, and contemporary fads that will quickly fade.

The material in the appendixes helps you implement ideas in the opening chapters. Appendix A provides a folktale and three puppet skits that include riddles. Use them independently or with bulletin boards in chapter 1, games in chapter 3, and puppets in chapter 5. Appendix B recommends riddle collections to buy and ways to save money when purchasing books to give away. Appendix C offers reproducibles and samples for bulletin boards in chapter 1, games in chapter 3, outreach ideas in chapter 4, and puppets in chapter 5; appendix C is also available on the book's website: www.ala.org/editions/extras/Anderson09577.

Please don't feel obligated to implement every idea or share every riddle in *Reading Is Funny!* The book contains a variety of material to suit a variety of tastes, not because I expect anyone to try them all. Pick the ideas that appeal to you and ignore the rest without guilt.

Because people who work with children often lack time and money, *Reading Is Funny!* suggests cheap, quick ways to carry out its ideas. Follow these directions, or elaborate on them. Treat all ideas as suggestions to inspire your creativity, not commandments to slavishly obey.

I've laughed a lot while writing *Reading Is Funny!* I hope you'll laugh a lot while reading it. I also hope you can use its contents to convince the children you work with that reading is funny!

PART ONE

WAYS TO SHARE RIDDLES WITH CHILDREN

1 Bulletin Boards That Promote Reading

Why did the silly librarian thumbtack baseball mitts to her bulletin board?

to "catch" patrons' eyes

Does your cork rectangle catch the eye or is it a bulletin "bored"? Putting riddles on it will enliven it—*and* put smiles on the faces of people who read it. It will also encourage reading. To make designs doable for colleagues with limited time or artistic ability, I've kept them fairly simple and included patterns that you can enlarge in appendix C. Feel free to draw your own patterns and embellish these ideas with touches of your own. Perhaps a gifted coworker, volunteer, or student would love to help. Lavish artwork isn't as important as your message that reading is funny!

FOR ALL BOARDS

- Although a possible caption for the top of each bulletin board follows its title, feel free to write your own.
- To make the point that reading is fun as well as funny, I always underline "Fun" in the caption "Reading Is Funny!" You may want to try this as well.
- To promote reading, incorporate book jackets into your bulletin boards. Use jackets of books related to the board's theme, new titles, or any books you like. (Write the books' call numbers on adhesive labels and attach them in the lower-left corner.) If directions call for pictures or cutouts in the middle of the board, add book jackets around the borders.

- Whenever directions call for book jackets, you can substitute pictures of book covers. Copy the covers of books on a color photocopier, or enlarge and print pictures of books off Amazon.com.
- Some bulletin boards feature book jackets in the middle and cutouts around the border. Enlarge patterns for cutouts in appendix C, or draw your own.
- Boldface 22-point type works well with riddles you'll glue onto book jackets and pictures from calendars or magazines.
- When keying riddles for cutouts into the computer, use boldface type big enough to read easily but small enough to fit inside the shapes. If necessary, vary line lengths to fit inside the shapes. (You can also print with marker right on the cutout.)
- Teacher stores and catalogs sell notepads in many shapes. You could use these instead of making cutouts.
- Display copies of pictured books near the board.
- The ideas for interactive bulletin boards help you adapt the earlier suggestions to start children thinking.

BULLETIN BOARDS FOR ANY TIME

Book Care: "Books Are Our Treasures. Let's Treasure Our Books."

Pick riddles under "Book Care" in chapter 7. Write an appropriate book-care tip for each.

For example:

> What would you call Cynthia Rylant's dog books if someone read them with dirty hands?
>
> Henry and "Smudge"
>
> Make sure your hands are clean before you read.

Key each riddle's question and answer into the computer in letters large enough to fill a page (or half a page for small bulletin boards). Make each tip fill a page as well. Place each tip underneath its corresponding riddle.

Book Jackets: "Reading Is Funny!"

For each book jacket find an appropriate riddle. (See chapter 8 as well as riddles on related subjects in other chapters.) You can also choose literacy riddles from chapter 7. Glue the riddles onto the book jackets before arranging the jackets on the board.

Animals: "Reading Is Funny!"

Gather animal pictures from old calendars and magazines. If their backgrounds are cluttered, cut around the animals and glue them onto plain paper. Glue on riddles that match from chapter 10, chapter 15, or other chapters, or choose appropriate riddles from chapter 13 to adapt these ideas for holidays. (See also "Picture Matching: 'Can You Fill In the Blanks?'" under "Interactive Bulletin Boards.")

People: "Reading Is Funny!"

Cut pictures of people out of catalogs, newspapers, and magazines, or use photos of willing coworkers or children. Glue on riddles. Choose appropriate riddles from chapter 13 to adapt these ideas for holidays, or match riddles to speakers (e.g., for athletes, see the riddles in chapter 14).

Talking Turnip Bulletin Board: "Look What's Talking!"

A European folktale inspired this bulletin board. (See "The Talking Turnip" in appendix A.) Find pictures that illustrate objects in chapter 15. Glue each talking pair onto a sheet of paper, with the object that answers the question on the right. Draw a dialogue balloon above each item. Write the question in the balloon above the left-hand object. Write its answer in the balloon above the object on the right.

Mysteries: "Track Down a Good Mystery"

Trace around your shoe and cut out eight to twelve copies of your footprint. Put a mystery riddle from chapter 8 on each footprint.

Space: "Reading Helps You Reach for the Stars" or "Be a Star: Read!"

Cut stars out of yellow paper or aluminum foil. On each, put a space riddle from chapter 16.

Sports: "Have a Ball: Read!"

Put riddles from chapter 14 on different kinds of ball cutouts.

SEASONAL BULLETIN BOARDS

Any Holiday: "Reading Is Funny!"

In the middle of your board, put a holiday poster, picture, or large cutout purchased from card shops or dollar stores. Frame this centerpiece with eight to twelve appropriate riddles from chapter 13. Key each riddle's question and answer into the computer in letters large enough to fill a page (or half a page for small bulletin boards).

Winter: "'Sno' Joke: Reading Is Funny!"

Cut snowflakes or snowmen out of white paper. Put a winter riddle from chapter 13 or a snow riddle from chapter 16 on each.

Valentine's Day: "You'll Love These Books"

Cut hearts out of red or pink paper. Put a valentine riddle from chapter 13 on each.

Easter: "'Hoppy' Easter!"

Cut eggs out of pastel paper. Put an Easter riddle from chapter 13 on each.

April: "April Showers Make Cozy Hours: Read!"

Cut raindrops out of light blue paper and umbrellas from any color. On each put a spring riddle from chapter 13 or a rain riddle from chapter 16.

Fall: "Fall into a Good Book"

Cut leaves out of red, yellow, and orange paper. Put a fall riddle from chapter 13 on each.

Halloween: "Treat Yourself to a Good Book" or "Scare Up a Good Book"

For "Treat Yourself to a Good Book," save empty candy bags. On each glue a riddle from chapter 12 or a Halloween riddle from chapter 13.

For "Scare Up a Good Book," enlarge and photocopy the ghost pattern in appendix C. On each ghost put ghost riddles from chapter 12 or Halloween riddles from chapter 13. A variation is to cut around riddles to make each resemble a dialogue balloon. Attach to the board so the riddles come from the ghosts' mouths.

Thanksgiving: "'Gobble' Up a Good Book"

Cut turkeys from brown paper. On each put a Thanksgiving riddle from chapter 13.

Christmas: "Merry Christmas!"

Cut a large tree out of green paper. (Enlarge the pattern in appendix C, or make a large triangle.) To make ornaments, trace around circular objects on construction paper or leftover wrapping paper. Cut them out. Glue a Christmas riddle from chapter 13 on each. Arrange them on the tree.

INTERACTIVE BULLETIN BOARDS

Interactive bulletin boards encourage children to match riddles to book jackets, pair questions to answers, figure out mystery words, or decode secret messages. Think of them as giant activity sheets and use sample activity sheets in appendix C to help you create your own.

When preparing interactive bulletin boards, put each question and each answer on a different sheet of paper, unless stated otherwise. Use type large enough to make the words fill each page (or half a page for small bulletin boards). Number each question. Unless directed otherwise, give each answer a different letter, but don't allow letters to correspond to the numbers of their questions. For example, don't assign *a* to the answer for the first question.

Under the caption of each interactive bulletin board, put directions telling children what to do. (Use the sample captions and directions here, or write your own.) When posting questions and answers, pretend an imaginary line runs down the middle of your board. Put all questions (or book jackets) in numerical order to the left of this dividing line; arrange all answers alphabetically on its right.

The number of riddles you use depends on how challenging you want your board to be. Four to eight riddles per board work well.

Answer keys let children see if they guessed right. To make a key, write the answers on an index card. Slip the card backward into an envelope. Write "Answers" on the back of the envelope. Attach the envelope to the board's lower-right-hand corner.

You can tie interactive bulletin boards into drawings to give away books. Children write their answers on paper and drop them into a box. (*Don't provide answer keys during drawings!*)

Consider handicapping this activity by age. Primary-grade children match any one or two questions to their answers. Children in intermediate grades match all four to eight. Consider offering a more developmentally appropriate alternative for preschoolers, such as activities copied from coloring books and children's magazines.

See "Riddle of the Week" in chapter 3 for more about drawings.

Using Captions

When making signs for the first four interactive bulletin boards, fill in the blanks (as shown below) with the appropriate words (for example, "book jacket," "riddle," "question," "answer," and "quote").

> ### CAN YOU GUESS?
>
> Match each _____ on the left to its _____ on the right.
>
> Check the answers in the envelope to see if you're right.
>
> Put answers back so others can check them.

Book Jackets: "Reading Is Funny!"

Children match book jackets to their related riddles.

Choose four to eight books. Number their jackets. Find a riddle to go with each book by checking chapter 8 or chapters with riddles related to the book's subject. (See chapter 10 for animal books, for example.)

Put each riddle's question *and* answer on a separate page, using type big enough to make the words fill the paper. Letter the riddles at random. (For example, make sure the riddle that corresponds to the first jacket isn't *a*.)

Any Holiday or Theme: "Reading Is Funny!"

Children match answers to the questions of riddles about an upcoming holiday or theme of your choice. For holidays, see chapter 13. For themes, see chapters with riddles related to the topic.

Loony Library: "Who Wrote That?"

Children decide who wrote each title in "The Loony Library," chapter 9's imaginary collection of silly books.

For the left side, cut book shapes out of construction paper. Put a different title on each. For the right side, put each author's name on a different page.

Talking Turnips: "Who Said That?"

Inspired by the folktale in appendix A, this bulletin board lets children imagine what inanimate objects might say if they could talk. Choose riddles from chapter 15.

Picture Matching: "Can You Fill In the Blanks?"

Make a sign like the one below to put under the caption.

> Read each question on the left.
>
> Find the picture on the right that fills in each blank.
>
> Check the answers in the envelope to see if you're right.
>
> Put answers back so others can check them.

For the right side, choose pictures from old magazines and calendars. If backgrounds are cluttered, cut out the desired animals or objects and glue them onto plain paper.

For the left side, find riddles that match the pictures by looking in chapters on related subjects. Make each riddle (both question *and* answer) fill a page, but put a line in place of the name of the animal or object. The following riddle would work for a picture of a kangaroo.

What would you get if you crossed a _____ with a clock?

a pocket watch

Mystery Word: "What Will You Find in the Library?"

By figuring out a mystery word, children discover that libraries contain treasures in this adaptation of the activity sheet "Why Should *You* Go to the Library?" in appendix C.

Put scrap paper and pencils near the board and make this sign to put under the question.

To answer the question, copy the underlined letters—in order—on a slip of paper.

Check the answer in the envelope to see if you're right.

Put the answer back so others can check it.

Look around the library and see if you can find some.

VARIATIONS

Use different questions and mystery words to introduce library rules and services.

What should library books never be?

overdue

What's new at the library?

a riddle jar

Post a riddle's question at the top of the board. Spell out its answer with the underlined letters. Riddles with short answers work best.

Secret Messages: "Crack the Code!"

Children can practice alphabet skills to decode answers to riddles if you make a bulletin board that looks like the "Crack the Code!" activity sheet in appendix C. Put scrap paper and pencils near the board. (See also "Crack the Code!" in chapter 3.)

2 Encouraging Children to Share Riddles

*How do you know when someone is sharing
a riddle with Mother Nature?*

The wind is "howling."

Children's love of riddles can be channeled into opportunities to practice reading for a purpose, speaking in front of a group, and writing with good penmanship, proper spelling, capitalization, and punctuation. The following activities encourage children to share riddles. Because children need a good supply of printed riddles, round up books and magazines like *Highlights* and *Ranger Rick*. Cut riddles from Sunday comics.

DAILY ANNOUNCEMENTS

Ask your principal to allow one or two students to conclude each day's announcements by reading a riddle. If possible, have readers visit the school library the day before to choose something from a book or the riddle file. To avoid bathroom humor and riddles that don't make sense, have children share their choices with you first.

Consider revolving the task among the classes on a regular rotation, for example, by grade level or alphabetically by teachers' last names. Each teacher can pick the student(s) who'll represent his or her class during its turn.

If every day seems like too much, consider doing this only once a week, perhaps Fridays.

ILLUSTRATED RIDDLES

HINT

Riddles posted outside the school cafeteria give children something to look at while waiting for lunch. Put up one to three riddles each week, depending on how many you receive.

For artwork that can be displayed on the bulletin board, around the library, or in the halls at school, children can illustrate riddles. Children write a riddle's question across the top of their paper and its answer across the bottom. In between they draw a picture to illustrate it. They sign their name in the lower-right-hand corner.

School librarians can have children illustrate riddles during class visits. In public libraries, consider making this activity part of a program that involves games from chapter 3 and the story or puppet skits in appendix A. (If you read "The Talking Turnip," children can illustrate riddles from chapter 15.)

Consider asking teachers to make this a class project. If they agree, let classes take turns displaying their artwork in the library.

"MINI HA-HA'S"

"Mini Ha-Ha's"—miniature riddle books—let children be authors. Children make these books by folding a sheet of paper into eight pages and copying riddles into it.

Before making "Mini Ha-Ha's" with children, practice till you have the steps down pat.

Give directions verbally while demonstrating. Children can fold their own papers as they watch you.

If you want to let children read for a purpose, make copies of the directions (shown opposite). Children can read them with you as you demonstrate or refer to them while working independently. In either case, circulate to help anyone having trouble.

HINTS

Turning the directions into a transparency or PowerPoint presentation saves paper.

For younger children, consider folding books ahead of time.

If time permits, let children read each other's "Mini Ha-Ha's" before taking them home.

Folding bigger paper gives more space for writing—and maybe illustrating—riddles.

"Mini Ha-Ha" instructions

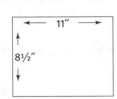 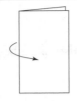

1. Hold your paper in front of you so it's wider than it is tall.

2. Fold it in half to bring the 8½" sides together.

3. Fold it in half again to bring the top and bottom edges together.

4. Fold it in half again to bring the 4¼" sides together.

 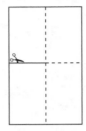 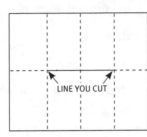 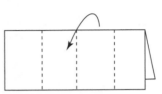

LINE YOU CUT

5. Open the paper so it looks the way it did in step 2.

6. Start from the folded edge. Tear (or cut) along the horizontal fold line you made in step 3. Stop when you reach the vertical fold you made in step 4.

7. Open your paper so it looks the way it did in step 1.

8. Fold it in half to bring the top and bottom edges together.

 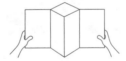 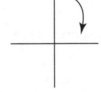 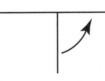

9. Hold the left edge between your left thumb and index finger. Hold the right edge between your right thumb and index finger.

10. Using both hands, push the edges toward each other to make a plus sign in the middle.

11. Fold the top of the plus sign down to meet the paper's right edge. Fold the bottom of the plus sign up to meet the right edge. Run your fingers down the center fold to crease it deeply.

12. Fold the left side over to make the cover. Crease the fold deeply.

13. Make up a title. Write it on the cover. Write your name on the cover as the author.

14. Write a riddle you like on each page. People won't laugh if they can't read your riddles, so write neatly, spell correctly, and leave a space between words.

15. Share your "Mini Ha-Ha" with family and friends.

From Dee Anderson, *Reading Is Funny!* (Chicago: ALA, 2009).

RIDDLE JAR

How to Make

Find a large plastic jar. (You can also use a bag, box, pail, or tin.) Make this sign to put on it.

> **RIDDLE JAR**
>
> You can give yourself some cheer:
>
> Take a riddle out of here.
>
> You can pass along a grin:
>
> Write new riddles; drop them in!

Make the following sign to display near the jar.

> People won't laugh at your riddle if they can't read it.
>
> Print neatly.
>
> Spell correctly.
>
> Leave a space between words.

Display the jar and the sign where the activity won't bother other people. Put pencils and slips of scrap paper nearby. Drop in a few riddles to start things off.

HINT

Introduce the jar in school libraries by explaining its use during each class's visit. In public libraries, tell patrons about it as they check out. Mention the jar in newsletters and on your website. Consider sending public service announcements to the media.

How to Use

Children can pull out a riddle when they visit the library. Encourage them to take it with them to share with family and friends later on. (I've noticed some children like to pull out riddles, read them, and then put them back in the jar. Although I hadn't anticipated this when I established the jar, it's fine with me. They're reading.)

If children want to share a riddle different from what they pulled out, they can write it on the scrap paper and drop it in. (Keeping a few riddle books near the jar might encourage this.)

If patrons take out more riddles than they put in, consider having volunteers or older children who are working off fines replenish the supply.

Variations

Put in riddles cut from Sunday comics and old magazines.

During October, fill a plastic pumpkin with riddles from chapter 12 or Halloween riddles from chapter 13.

During December, fill a gift-wrapped box with Christmas riddles from chapter 13.

During March, fill a striped hat with Dr. Seuss riddles from chapter 8.

Fill a gift-wrapped box or sturdy gift bag with birthday riddles from chapter 11. Let children choose a riddle on their birthdays.

WAYS TO USE CHILDREN'S RIDDLES

Collecting Riddles from Children

Get a large unbreakable container, index cards, pencils or pens, and boxes for filing the cards. Make a sign to display near your container.

MAKE US LAUGH: SHARE YOUR FAVORITE RIDDLES

Write your favorite riddle on an index card.

Please start writing on the second line.

Write your first and last names at the bottom.

We won't laugh if we can't read your riddle.

Please print neatly.
Spell words correctly.
Leave a space between words.

Put your riddle in the [specify what kind of container you have]. *Please don't fold it!*

We'll share our favorite riddles [tell how *you* plan to use the riddles].

Put the container and sign in a prominent place that's easily accessible. Set cards and pencils or pens near them. To model what children should do, write a riddle and your name on a card. Attach your sample to the container.

Empty the container periodically and file the riddles in a box. (See chapter 6.) Check this file when you need riddles, such as for the following projects.

Note: When sharing children's riddles, write the names of the kids who submitted them underneath.

Bookmarks

To create riddle bookmarks, set up your page to make three columns. Key in riddles from the file.

After filling the first column, copy and paste the material into each of the other two columns. Make another master sheet for the back. Add more riddles, share information about your library, or recommend books.

Put three fronts on one master sheet and three backs on another. Print one-third as many copies as you need. (If you want 300 bookmarks, print 100 copies.)

Cut apart the bookmarks. Put them at the circulation desk, or distribute them outside your library. (See chapter 4 for possible distribution points. See appendix C for sample bookmarks.)

Bulletin Boards

See chapter 1.

Newspapers, Newsletters, and Websites

Submit riddles for each issue of your school's newspaper.

Submit riddles for each library and school newsletter. Introduce your first riddle column with a brief note to parents. Encourage them to share the humor with their children, and explain the benefits of riddles. (Consider listing the introduction's first six reasons for sharing riddles.)

Post riddles on your home page. Change weekly or monthly.

3 Games to Play with Riddles

Why do deer enjoy playing checkers?
They're "game" animals.

Children are game animals, too, because they love to play. Child's play isn't all fun and games, however. It's also educational. Playing games from this chapter helps children learn while having fun.

These games exercise children's brains as kids figure out answers to riddles, learn new vocabulary, and think about the multiple meanings of words. They also let children read for a purpose and develop the lifetime skill of finding books in a library.

You can play the quiet and active games anywhere, for example, during library programs, indoor recess, and class parties. Choosing appropriate riddles makes the games fit any holiday or theme.

Be flexible because a game that delights one group might flop with another. Prepare more games than you can use in the allotted time; then follow the children's lead. If they're really enjoying a game, extend it. If they're not, drop it and move on to another.

If the games don't work for you, change these directions. These rules were made to be broken!

Do these games give you a feeling of déjà vu? No wonder, because I simply incorporated riddles into familiar games. What games can *you* adapt to include riddles?

QUIET GAMES

Quiet games work best if children play in groups of four to six. If possible, have a volunteer play with each group. Explain rules to helpers beforehand so they can teach children.

If you can't get help, explain the rules to everyone before dividing into groups. Circulate to see how each group is faring.

Card Games

Appendix C provides two reproducible decks of cards. The Talking Turnip deck features questions and quotes. (For example, "What did the scissors say to the hair?" "It won't be long now.") You can play with these cards independently or after reading "The Talking Turnip" in appendix A or *Talk, Talk: An Ashanti Legend*, its African counterpart, by Deborah M. Newton Chocolate.

The Loony Library deck features silly, imaginary titles by pretend authors. For example, "Who wrote *The Little Tattletale*? I. Will Tell."

You can use each deck to play three different card games. Although these directions use the Talking Turnip cards as examples, you can also play all three games by matching Loony Library titles and authors' names. (To use either deck with an active game, see "Find Your Partner.")

HOW TO PREPARE FOR ALL CARD GAMES

Photocopy the Talking Turnip cards in appendix C to make a deck for each group. Don't cut several sheets at once.

You can keep the game fresher by making additional decks with different riddles. Groups can switch decks for each round.

To make additional decks, write each question and each answer in ink on an index card, or key the material into the computer. Print on card stock or on labels to attach to index cards. Divide into decks of eight to thirteen pairs. (Having eight pairs shortens the game for younger children. Playing with thirteen pairs might work better for a group of six.) Give each deck an extra card that says "You Win!" if you're playing Talking Turnip.

TALKING TURNIP AND LOONY LIBRARY

Play Talking Turnip or Loony Library the way you'd play Old Maid, but match questions to quotes instead of identical pairs. A twist at the end allows the player holding the last card to win.

Mix up all the cards.

One child deals out all the cards, one at a time, facedown.

Players look at their cards and check for corresponding questions and quotes. Those who find such matches in their hands read aloud the words on those cards before placing them faceup in front of them.

All players hold their unmatched cards so no one else can see them.

Without peeking, the player on the dealer's left takes one card from the dealer's hand.

If it corresponds to a card he already has, the player reads aloud both question and quote and puts the cards down in front of him.

If the drawn card doesn't correspond, the player keeps it and lets the child on his left take a card from him.

Keep playing until all questions have been matched to their quotes. Whoever is holding the turnip card wins.

RIDDLE ROUNDUP

Play Riddle Roundup like Concentration (aka Memory), but search for corresponding questions and quotes instead of identical pairs.

The dealer removes the turnip card and lays the other cards facedown in rows of five to six cards each.

The player on the dealer's left starts by flipping over any two cards and reading them aloud.

If they are a question and its quote, the player lays them faceup in front of her.

The player may then flip over any other two cards.

If they are not a question and its quote, she flips them back facedown.

Then the next player takes a turn.

Keep playing until children have matched all the cards.

The child who matched the most questions to their corresponding quotes wins.

HINT FOR BOTH GAMES

If you want to make matching questions and answers easier for younger children, give each question and its answer the same number.

Who Said That? and Who Wrote That?

In this noncompetitive game, children work as a group to match questions to quotes. Put cards in the middle of the playing area. Keep questions in one pile and quotes in another.

Children take turns picking the top question. After reading it aloud, they lay each card down faceup to make a vertical column. After they've read all the questions, children take turns picking the top quote and reading it aloud. Then everyone decides which question the quote answers. The player who read the card lays it down next to the appropriate question.

HINT

If children have trouble matching a card—or you know their answer is wrong—suggest they put it aside. Point out that the answer might be clearer after reading more cards.

Crack the Code!

Children practice alphabet skills to decode answers to riddles in this variation of a bulletin board in chapter 1 and an outreach activity in chapter 4.

Consider introducing this noncompetitive game by showing your code books or reading a detective story. (Each title in James Preller's Jigsaw Jones series includes a code.)

Write different riddles on index cards, one per card. (Riddles with short answers work best.) Write the letter that comes *before* each letter in the answer. For example, "the" becomes "sgd." (See the Crack the Code! activity sheet in appendix C.)

Distribute index cards, scrap paper, and pencils.

Tell children to write on their scrap paper the letter that comes *after* each letter in their riddle's answer. When all children have decoded their answers, they pass their cards to their left. Play until interest flags or time runs out.

> **HINT**
>
> If you use a different code, post a copy where children can see it.

Activity Sheets

Make copies of any activity sheet in appendix C for each child or small group. Consider saving paper by turning the sheets into transparencies or PowerPoint presentations for everyone to figure out together.

Get It Together

Children put together puzzles to read riddles in this noncompetitive game.

HOW TO PREPARE

Pick as many riddles as you'll have players. Key each into the computer in letters large enough to fill a page. Print on card stock.

Cut each riddle into six pieces. Make each puzzle different. Put each puzzle's pieces in an envelope or Ziploc bag.

HOW TO PLAY

Give everyone a puzzle. At a signal, children assemble their puzzles and read the riddles to themselves. Let children take apart puzzles and pass them to their left as long as interest lasts.

> **HINT**
>
> Number each riddle. Write its number on the envelope or bag *and* on the back of each piece. This makes reassembling puzzles easier if children mix up pieces from different envelopes.

ACTIVE GAMES

Find Your Partner

Find Your Partner provides a noncompetitive, mobile way to match corresponding Talking Turnip and Loony Library cards. Consider introducing this game with a story about two friends, for example, Arnold Lobel's Frog and Toad stories or the Miggs and Jiggs puppet skits in appendix A.

HOW TO PREPARE

Photocopy the cards in appendix C to provide one card per child. For more than twenty-seven children, make duplicates of either deck, or play with both Loony Library and Talking Turnip cards.

HOW TO PLAY

Give every child a card. Tell them to find the person with the other half of their riddle and sit down together when they have. Check seated players. If their cards go together, congratulate them. If the cards don't correspond, tell children to keep looking. When everyone has paired up successfully, players take turns reading aloud their cards.

HINTS

To simplify for younger children (or a large number of players) divide the children into small groups before distributing cards.

If an odd number is playing, take a card so you can be somebody's partner.

Egg Hunt

Egg Hunt combines the fun of looking for hidden objects with the pleasure of reading riddles.

HOW TO PREPARE

Play this game around Easter or after reading an egg story. Write egg riddles from chapter 16 on slips of paper. Or key riddles into the computer and cut them apart. Put each in a plastic pop-apart egg. Make at least as many eggs as you have searchers.

Hide the eggs so children can find them without moving anything. Provide a bag or other container to hold the eggs.

HOW TO PLAY

Children put eggs into the container as they find them. Count eggs as children deposit them so you'll know when they've found them all.

Sit around the container. Children take turns opening an egg and reading aloud its riddle. (Time permitting, let children try to guess answers before they're read aloud.)

HINT

To let everyone read, divide large groups into small ones. Give each group a supply of eggs. Children take turns opening eggs and reading riddles within these small groups.

Pass It On

Nobody has to drop out of this noncompetitive variation of Hot Potato. Whoever is holding the object when the music stops gets to read a riddle to the group.

HOW TO PREPARE

Write ten to twelve riddles on slips of paper, or key them into the computer, print, and cut them apart. Fold each in half and drop all of them into an unbreakable container.

HOW TO PLAY

Children stand in a circle and pass the container while you play a recording. When you stop the music, whoever has the container pulls out a riddle and reads it aloud. (Time permitting, let children try to guess answers before they're read aloud.)

Start the music and pass the container around again. Play until interest lags, you've read all the riddles, or time runs out.

VARIATION

Pass around a beanbag, Nerf ball, or sponge. When the music stops, the player with the object reads a riddle from the container. During each round, children pass the object in a different way (e.g., counterclockwise, over their heads, between their legs, etc.). Children can suggest different ways to pass the object.

The Toll-Bridge Troll Game

Inspired by Patricia Rae Wolff's *The Toll-Bridge Troll*, this game encourages children to outwit a troll by answering riddles to cross an imaginary bridge. Read the funny picture book before you play, or present its Halloween puppet version, "The Ghost Bridge," in appendix A.

HOW TO PREPARE

Choose as many riddles as you'll have players plus extras in case some are too hard. Write each riddle—*and* its answer—in ink on a separate index card, or enter each into the computer. Print on card stock or on labels to attach to index cards. (If you've tried activities in chapter 6, you might already have a supply of cards you can use.)

Pick riddles children can probably figure out. Hink pinks and riddles with answers that involve anagrams and homophones work best.

Hink pinks have words that rhyme as their answers. Make up your own, or choose riddles from Francis X. McCall's *A Huge Hog Is a Big Pig* or Marilyn Burns's *The Hink Pink Book*.

Anagram riddles use the letters of one word to spell another. Create your own (see chapter 6), or pick anagram riddles from Joanne E. Bernstein's *Fiddle with a Riddle*.

Homophone riddles have answers with words that sound alike but are spelled differently. Make up your own, or select riddles from Marvin Terban's *Eight Ate*.

If you don't want to prepare index cards, read riddles right out of the books.

HOW TO PLAY

Have children line up along one wall. Explain that you are a troll who won't let them cross your bridge unless they answer your riddles.

Starting at the head of the line, ask each child in turn a riddle. Give hints if necessary. If someone can't answer, ask her another question.

When a child has successfully answered a riddle, she may cross the bridge (i.e., move to the other side of the room). Everyone must move in a different way! Encourage creativity.

VARIATION

Divide children into two teams—the Trolls and the Triggs. Teams sit in rows facing each other. Each gets a pile of riddles.

The first child on the Triggs team reads aloud the riddle on the top card on the team's pile. The Trolls may confer for thirty to sixty seconds. If they can answer, they earn a point. If the Trolls can't answer, neither side scores. Either way, the Trigg discards the riddle.

Now the first child on the Trolls team reads aloud the riddle on the top card on the team's pile. The Triggs confer for thirty to sixty seconds. If they can answer, they earn a point. If the Triggs can't answer, neither side scores. Either way, the Troll discards the riddle.

Teams alternate asking and answering questions until they've read all the cards, time runs out, or interest lags. Each child should get a turn to read. The side scoring the most points wins.

> **HINT**
>
> To give everyone a turn to read, divide large groups of children into four teams—two Triggs and two Trolls.

GAMES THAT TEACH LIBRARY SKILLS

Riddle of the Week

Each week think of a book, author, subject, or location you want children to know. Pick any riddle, or find a related one.

Think of a clue that hints at your subject. For example, introduce children to the unabridged dictionary by writing, "Find the answer next to the big book that tells what words mean." (Call numbers can be clues, too, for example, "Find the answer near books with call number 567.9.")

HINT

If you'd rather not use the computer, print the question and clue on a chalkboard or whiteboard. Print the answer on paper small enough to fit on the front of a shelf.

Key the question and clue into the computer using a large type size.

Use boldface 18-point type to key in the answer at the bottom of the page.

Print the page and cut off the answer.

Post the question and clue in a prominent spot under the heading "Riddle of the Week." Tape the answer near the featured book(s).

If every week seems like too much, do this during Children's Book Week, the week of Dr. Seuss's birthday, National Library Week, and your summer reading program.

GIVE AWAY BOOKS IN A DRAWING

To tie this activity into a drawing, have children write the answer on paper along with their names and contact information. (In a school, have them write their teacher's name. In a public library, get their phone number.) They drop their answers into a container that sits in a prominent place.

The number of winners and the frequency of your drawings depend on the number of available books. (Our school held monthly drawings; therefore, children who found the answer every week had four chances to win a book each time.) To buy riddle books cheaply, see appendix B.

Some children might know or be able to guess the answers. To make sure they found what you hid, capitalize and underline random letters:

Where can pigs fly?

At The "aiR-por<u>k</u>"

Children must copy the answer *exactly* as you wrote it. Save each answer after taking it down. When pulling slips, discard those whose answers don't match your original.

I posted the following sign next to the weekly question and clue. Adapt the wording to fit your library.

FIND THE RIDDLE'S ANSWER, AND YOU MIGHT WIN A FREE BOOK!

Use the clue to find the answer to the riddle.

On scrap paper, copy the answer down *exactly* the way it looks.

Write your name and your teacher's name on the paper.

Put your answer in the jar near the door.

You must copy the answer exactly to win the drawing.

Put in only one answer each week.

The Loony Library Book Hunt

The Loony Library Book Hunt uses the imaginary collection of silly titles in chapter 9 to teach children, step-by-step, how to find books in your library.

Spread the five activities below over a number of library visits. Practice the first activity until children breeze through it. Then move to the next level.

Having more than one person verify children's answers makes the activities run more smoothly. If you have no coworkers or volunteers to help, consider working with one small group of children at a time while the other children read independently.

HOW TO PREPARE FOR THE FIRST FOUR ACTIVITIES

For the first four activities, print each title and its author's name on a large index card. Make the call number large enough to read from a distance. Or use large, boldface type on a computer and print on card stock.

Note: If you classify beginning readers as ER or EZ, change some Loony Library call numbers from E to ER or EZ.

HOW TO PREPARE FOR THE LAST ACTIVITY

For the last activity, put each title and each author's name on a separate card. *Don't write call numbers!*

Put scrap paper and pencils by your catalog, if they're not already there.

For card catalogs. Make an author and title card for each book. Both should give title, author, and call number. Type "This Isn't Real" on each card.

For automated catalogs. For each book add a pretend entry with title, author, and call number. Enter "This Isn't Real" in the publisher's space. Make *Loony Library* a subject heading. If you use different material types, create a new category.

HOW TO PLAY

1. Learning What Call Numbers Represent. Each child gets a card and decides what type of book it is. Ask children who have fiction books to stand. Check their cards. If children have fiction, congratulate them for being right. If they don't, ask them to sit. When you've checked all cards, ask everyone to sit. Repeat with easies, nonfiction, and biographies. (If you classify beginning readers as ER or EZ, ask children with those cards to stand as well.)

2. Finding the Section for Each Call Number. Each child gets a card, decides what type of book it is, and goes to the section where that type of book is shelved. He then raises his hand and waits for someone to check his card. Congratulate children who are right. Help others figure out where to go.

(Children don't need to find their books on the shelf. They just need to stand in the appropriate section.)

3. Learning Shelf Order. Follow the above steps. When everyone has found the appropriate section, have the children in each location stand in shelf order. For example, children line up alphabetically by the authors' last names in the sections with easies, beginning readers, and fiction. Children with biographies line up alphabetically by the subjects' last names. Children with nonfiction line up numerically by the call numbers. Congratulate groups that lined up correctly. Help children who are out of order make corrections.

4. Using Call Numbers to Find Books. Give each child a card. Children slide their cards between the books where the Loony Library title would be if it were real and raise their hands so someone can check their work. Demonstrate. As hands go up, check cards. Congratulate children who are right. Help those who are wrong or confused. After finding their correct locations, children can help classmates or read quietly.

5. Using the Catalog to Find Books. Model looking up books and writing down their call numbers on scrap paper. Then give each child either an author *or* title card. They must search the catalog for their title or author before looking for their book's location, following the procedure above. *Remind them not to write on the cards, so you can reuse them.*

HINT

When working with one small group, give all children the same type of book so they can practice lining up in shelf order.

4 Using Riddles for Public Relations

Why did the silly librarian write public service announcements with peanut butter?

> *to "spread" the word*

Although writing with peanut butter is silly, spreading the word about your library's treasures and services is smart. Besides sending public service announcements to the media, you can go out into the community and entice people to use the library.

Consider spreading the word by distributing literature through places that families frequent and setting up informational booths at community events. Riddles can help you grab people's attention in either case. Because they also show that its staff has a sense of humor, riddles make the library seem more inviting.

DISTRIBUTE BOOKMARKS THROUGH PLACES FAMILIES VISIT

Think about the many places in your community that families visit, either regularly (like dentists' offices) or seasonally (like pumpkin patches).

Ask these places if they'll distribute PR materials advertising your services. If they agree, ask how many they want. Take your regular literature, or design bookmarks tailored to their focus. (See chapter 2 for directions on making bookmarks. See appendix C for samples geared to offices of dentists, physicians, and eye doctors; pet stores and animal shelters; and pumpkin patches.)

When delivering materials, ask distributors to call if they want more. Consider checking back periodically to see if distributors have run out.

INFORMATIONAL BOOTHS AT COMMUNITY EVENTS

Participate in events where organizations can set up booths. People stride past displays of pamphlets and books but might stop for children's activities.

Talk to adults about library services while their children assemble puzzles, create puppets, or decode secret messages. When people leave, urge them to visit the library soon.

Make available literature about your library. To intrigue folks into reading your PR instead of pitching it as "litter-ature," let the sample activity sheets and bookmarks in appendix C inspire you to create handouts that are standouts.

Puzzles

WHAT YOU NEED

riddles, card stock, scissors, envelopes or Ziploc bags; optional: labels

HOW TO PREPARE

Key a riddle into the computer in letters almost large enough to fill a page. In smaller letters at the bottom of the page, include a message like "Find more riddles at [your library's name]. Please visit soon." Print enough copies on card stock for the expected attendance. (Preparing three to five different riddles encourages more reading.)

Create a sign that says "Make Your Own Puzzle." Cut a riddle into five to eight pieces and attach it around the sign's border.

Consider printing labels that read "Puzzled? Find answers at [your library's name, address, phone number, and website]."

DURING THE EVENT

Put up the sign and lay out the materials. Ask children who pass by, "Would you like to make a puzzle?" If they stop, give them a riddle. If you prepared several, let them choose one.

Tell them to cut their paper into five to eight pieces. Give them an envelope or plastic bag for their pieces. (Attach a "Puzzled?" label, if you made any.)

Paper Bag Puppets

WHAT YOU NEED

paper lunch sacks, crayons or markers, sheets of riddles, bottles of glue or glue sticks

HOW TO PREPARE

Make enough copies of the reproducible library riddles in appendix C for the expected attendance.

Print half as many papers as you'll need. If you expect 200 visitors, make 100 copies. Cut each sheet in half. Glue one section of riddles to the back of each sack.

Make a sign that says "Make Your Own Puppet." Make a puppet. (See "Paper Bag Puppets" in chapter 5.) Attach the puppet to the sign.

DURING THE EVENT

Put up your sign. Space three to five piles of crayons along the table within children's reach. Put bags near you.

Ask children who pass by, "Would you like to make a puppet?" If they stop, point out the crayons and give them a bag. Show them the riddles on the back. Encourage children to share the riddles with others.

Consider donning a puppet and asking children some riddles.

Decode Secret Messages

WHAT YOU NEED

poster board, scrap paper, pencils

HOW TO PREPARE

Make one of the activity sheets in appendix C into a poster. (See "Crack the Code!" or "Why Should *You* Go to the Library?")

DURING THE EVENT

Set up the poster so children can see it. Put pencils and scrap paper nearby.

Ask children who pass by, "Do you want to figure out secret messages?" If they stop, give them paper and pencil. Explain how to figure out the answers.

Congratulate children when they finish. Encourage them to share the riddles.

VARIATION

Make copies of either sheet. Print information about your library on the back. (See samples in appendix C for ideas.) Point out the information when you hand out the sheets.

Read a Riddle

WHAT YOU NEED

poster board, book pockets or envelopes, index cards

HOW TO PREPARE

Turn the poster board on its longer side. Write "Your Library Has Lots of Laughs" across the top. Across the bottom write "You'll Find More Riddles at Your Library. Please Visit Soon."

In between, glue six to twelve book pockets (or envelopes cut in half). Key as many riddles as you have pockets into the computer in 18-point type. Cut apart questions and answers. Glue one question on each pocket. Glue one answer near the bottom of each index card. (Turn cards on their sides so they'll fit the pockets.) Put each answer in the appropriate pocket.

DURING THE EVENT

Display the poster within children's reach. Tape the poster securely to the side of a large box weighted with heavy books to keep little hands from knocking it over.

Ask children who pass by, "Would you like to read riddles?" If they stop, demonstrate reading the questions on the pockets and pulling out the answers.

5 Sharing Riddles through Puppets

What would you get if you crossed a top with the storybook puppet that came to life?

"Spin-occhio" (Pinocchio)

Pinocchio isn't the only puppet that came to life. Even the humblest homemade creation seems real in the eyes of a child. One morning I made paper bag puppets with the boys I was babysitting. Shortly after that, the younger one was picking at his lunch.

Impulsively, I slipped on one of the puppets, turned it toward him, and said, "Eat your food, Justin. It's good for you." Immediately, his older brother begged, "Make it talk to me! Make it talk to me!"

Because children relate to puppets so well, teaming puppets with riddles makes a winning combination.

MAKE PUPPETS WITH CHILDREN

Encourage children to share riddles with other people by having them create the simple puppets below and gluing on their backs appropriate riddles from appendix C. Sharing riddles as a puppeteer gives children a purpose for reading and lets them reread the same material many times, which improves fluency. Talking through puppets can help shy children share riddles more comfortably.

The library-related riddles in appendix C work with any animal, person, or fantasy creature that children choose to make. The other three pages work with dish, ghost, and snowmen puppets, respectively.

Because each page has riddles for two puppets, make half as many copies as you have children (e.g., make twelve copies for twenty-four children). Cut each sheet in half.

Dish and Spoon Puppets for Mother Goose Riddles

Draw faces on the backs of plastic spoons with permanent markers, or trace around a milk jug lid on paper. Draw a face on it, cut it out, and tape it to the spoon. If you don't have spoons, cut some out of cardboard.

Draw a face on a paper plate. Make a handle by taping an ice-cream stick or strip of cardboard to the back.

Paper Bag Puppets

Lay a lunch sack in front of you with the flat bottom at the top. Draw a face on the bottom. Draw a body on the front.

Slide your hand inside. Lay your thumb against your palm and bend your fingers down into the flat bottom.

Move your fingertips forward and back toward your palm. Voilà! The puppet talks.

VARIATIONS

Cut features, arms, and clothes from colored paper, wrapping paper, or fabric scraps.

Make ghost puppets at Halloween.

Make snowman puppets in winter.

Make puppets to act out Patricia Rae Wolff's *The Toll-Bridge Troll*.

After reading the book, let children make Trigg and Troll puppets. To encourage them to act out the story at home, key Trigg's riddles into the computer. Print a copy for each child to glue on the back of his puppet.

ASK RIDDLES WITH PUPPETS

Use puppets to ask children riddles. Puppets with movable mouths work best. (If you use only one puppet to ask riddles, its appearance lets children know what to expect.)

PRESENT SKITS WITH PUPPETS

Appendix A contains three puppet skits featuring riddles. Use them independently or as part of programs that include playing games (see chapter 3) or making up riddles (see chapter 6).

Any two puppets can play the parts of Miggs and Jiggs. To create additional skits for them, pick riddles that Miggs can ask and make up silly things for Jiggs to say. Think literally, the way Amelia Bedelia does. Or ask young children riddles and incorporate their answers into Jiggs's dialogue. One day, for example, I asked second-graders, "A penny and a quarter sat on a bridge. The penny jumped off. Why didn't the quarter?" One girl said, "It didn't have legs." Her reply went into "The Punch Line."

Veteran puppeteers can turn to the skits in appendix A. If you've never worked with puppets before, however, you might find the following information helpful.

Basic Tips for Presenting Puppet Skits

- Don't let the technical wizardry of television's Muppets intimidate you! You don't need to be anywhere near that good. Children like puppets so much, they enjoy even the simplest performances.
- Do the same things you do when reading stories aloud. For example, speak clearly and loudly enough to make yourself understood. Practicing a little ahead of time helps you deliver lines with appropriate expression. If children react to something funny, wait till their laughter dies down before going on.
- You don't need a stage to perform these skits, because children look at the puppets, not you. Sit on a chair or stool and lay a large, flat box (like what the post office sells for mailing packages) across your lap when you need a place to rest your props. (If you don't have time to memorize the dialogue, thumbtack photocopied pages of the skit to this box for easy reference.)
- Seat children directly in front of you. If they sit too far off to either side, they'll miss some of the action. Make sure, however, that you have enough room to manipulate puppets without hitting members of your audience!
- You can perform all three skits by yourself, or ask someone else to play one of the parts.
- Put your hands all the way inside the puppets so they won't fall off.
- To show off the faces of puppets with movable mouths, bend down your wrist. To give puppets with movable arms good posture, hold your arm straight up from the elbow.
- Turn the puppets slightly toward each other in what's called "three-quarters position." This makes characters look as if they're talking to each other, not to the audience, and lets children see three-fourths of the puppets' faces.
- Move only the puppet that's talking. Hold the other puppet so that it pays attention to the speaker.
- Make puppets nod to agree with something and shake their heads to disagree. Exaggerate their actions to make children laugh.

- Consider using a silly voice for Jiggs.
- Reverse the scripts' stage directions, if necessary. For example, work the child in "The Ghost Bridge" on your left hand if you write with that hand. I work Jiggs on my right hand, because my puppet feels better there. The opposite might be true in your case.
- If you make a mistake, quickly correct yourself and keep going. The audience members might not even notice your goof, because they can't read the script.
- You might feel awkward at first. I did. The more you work with puppets, however, the more comfortable you'll become, especially when you hear children's laughter and their eager question, "Are we going to have puppets today?"

Acquiring Puppets

If you don't have puppets, you can buy them through some teacher- and library-supply catalogs as well as in some department, dollar, and toy stores. Puppets in good condition sometimes show up at yard sales and thrift shops.

You can also make simple puppets out of socks and mittens. Wiggly eyes, buttons, little pompons, sequins, and circles cut from paper or felt make good eyes and noses. Attach these with hot glue on the back of a mitten or near the toe of a sock. Yarn works well for hair.

To operate, bend your wrist down to show off the face. Keep moving your fingers and thumb away from each other. Voilà! The puppet talks. (Sock puppets work better if you first push some of the material in the toe all the way back to your palm.)

See my book *Amazingly Easy Puppet Plays* for more details about presenting simple puppet skits and making puppets out of socks and mittens. (Although this book is out of print, you can borrow copies on interlibrary loan.) Sock puppets with movable arms work for "The Ghost Bridge," in appendix A.

To create more elaborate puppets, look for library books on sewing (646.4) and puppets (745.59 and 791.5).

6 Do It Yourself!

How to Make Up Riddles and Keep a Riddle File

What would you call a bookcase you have to put together without any help?

> *a do-it-"your-shelf" project*

Creating riddles isn't as hard as you might think, and it can amuse you while you're commuting or performing mundane tasks like washing dishes. The more riddles you read and the more you make up your own, the easier it gets—and the better you get.

These tips and examples can help you start.

CREATING SPIN-OFFS

Think of Words That Rhyme with a Word (or Part of a Word) in a Riddle's Answer

What has eight arms, lives in the ocean, and tells time?
> a "clock-topus"

What can bang on your door with eight arms?
> a "knock-topus"

Think of Other Words and Phrases That Use the Funny Part of an Answer

What do antelopes read every day?
> the "gnus-paper"

What do antelopes get for the first day of school?
> "gnu" clothes

Think of Situations That Can Use the Same Punch Line

> Why are the teeth scared to go to the dentist?
>> They're "yellow."

> Why are the baby goldfinches afraid to fly?

> Why are the maple leaves afraid to fall off the tree?

MAKING UP NEW RIDDLES

Start with the punch line; then think of a question that leads to it. These eight suggestions can help you make up funny answers.

1. Think of Idioms

The figure of speech becomes either the whole punch line or part of it. The question can explain the figurative meaning and perhaps invoke some of its literal aspects.

> Why is it hard to talk when your kitten bites the middle of your sneaker?
>> The cat's got your "tongue."

Or include the idiom in the question and answer it with the literal interpretation.

> How did the silly twins try to make time fly the week before their birthday?
>> They threw a clock out the window.

2. Think of Words or Phrases with More Than One Meaning

> Why did the silly kids bring dynamite to their friend's birthday party?
>> They'd been asked to help "blow up" balloons.

3. Think of Homophones (Words That Sound Alike but Are Spelled Differently)

> What did Little Jack Horner eat in geometry class?
>> his Christmas "pi"

4. Think of Names of Places, People, and Storybook Characters

Look for little words inside their names.

What author makes good sandwiches?
Cynthia "Rye-lant"

Or play with words that sound like their names.

What would you get if you crossed a spinning dreidel with Mickey Mouse's creator?
Walt "Dizzy"

Or think of longer words that contain part of these names.

Who likes honey, has a friend named Christopher Robin, and can disappear without a trace?
Winnie-the-"Poof"

5. Work with Words or Phrases You Come Across That Sound Like Punch Lines

Seeing a sign for "Whirlpool" led to this riddle:

Where do ballerinas go swimming?
"twirl-pools"

6. Let the Comics Inspire You

While pretending to be a wizard, the cat in Patrick McDonnell's *Mutts* called his dictionary "my magic book of shpells [*sic*]." That inspired this riddle:

Why does Harry Potter carry around a dictionary?
It helps him "spell."

7. Rewrite Jokes in Riddle Form

Mom: "Why didn't you take out the garbage?"
Son: "It already had a date."

When don't you have to take out your garbage?
when it already has a date

8. Use a Punch Line in Different Contexts

> Why can't you take out a reference book?
> It already has a date.

MAKING UP RIDDLES WITH CHILDREN

Anagrams

In *Fiddle with a Riddle*, Joanne E. Bernstein describes how she creates riddles with children.

Think of a three- or four-letter word (e.g., "TOPS"). Rearrange its letters to make a new word (e.g., "SPOT"). Make up a definition for the anagram (e.g., "something on a leopard's coat").

> Make TOPS into something on a leopard's coat.
>
> SPOT

If children write their anagrams on index cards, you can use them to play the Toll-Bridge Troll Game in chapter 3.

Hink Pinks

Think of two words that rhyme and make up a definition for them.

Introduce hink pinks by reading Francis X. McCall's *A Huge Hog Is a Big Pig* or a few riddles from Marilyn Burns's *The Hink Pink Book*. Let children use rhyming dictionaries, if you have them.

If children write their hink pinks on index cards, you can use them to play the Toll-Bridge Troll Game in chapter 3.

Pattern Riddles

Pattern riddles have answers containing the same word or syllable, like the "spirit" riddles under "Ghosts" in chapter 12. Knowing the answer to one riddle in a series helps children figure out the others. It also allows them to make up similar riddles.

Suggestions for creating new riddles based on patterns occur throughout *Reading Is Funny!*

Read more about making up riddles in Joanne E. Bernstein's *Fiddle with a Riddle*, Marvin Terban's *Funny You Should Ask*, and Mike Thaler's *Funny Side Up!*

KEEPING A RIDDLE FILE

Write riddles you like on index cards. Write an appropriate subject heading at the top of each card. For example, either "Doctors" or "Food" makes a good subject heading for this riddle.

> Why did the doctor send the ham home from the hospital?
>
> It was "cured."

Choose which heading you'd be most likely to use, or put "Doctors" on the original card. Copy the riddle onto a new card labeled "Food." File cards alphabetically by subject in a box.

To save space, add new riddles to cards in the box. When the originals fill up, start new cards with the same subject headings.

Variation

To collect riddles from children, see "Ways to Use Children's Riddles" in chapter 2.

If you're technologically savvy, create a riddle database.

PART TWO

THE RIDDLES

7 Laugh Lines
Riddles about Literacy

AUTHORS

In General

If desired, use names of individual authors.

What happened when the author sent her editor a manuscript written on flypaper?

He couldn't put it down.

Why is the author writing on sandpaper?

It's a "rough" draft.

Why was the room chilly while the author wrote the first copy of a new book?

It had a "draft."

What did the author call the first [or preliminary] copy of his dog story?

a "ruff" draft

How is the author's story coming along?

"all write"

What will you always get if you ask authors about their work?

"write" answers

What do authors need to succeed?

the "write" stuff

What authors make up the scariest stories?

"ghost-writers"

What did the judge do when sentencing the author for plagiarism?

She "threw the book" at him.

Why do fiction authors look strange?

"Tales" grow out of their heads.

How are authors of heartwarming stories like happy dogs?

Their "tales" are "moving."

Why can't frogs and toads be authors?

They have no "tales."

Why did the silly writer visit the cemetery to get ideas?

It had lots of "plots."

Why was the author's head wet?

She'd gotten a "brainstorm."

Why did the author take a dictionary to the park?

He liked playing with words.

Why does the author write "Bic" when he autographs books?

It's his "pen" name.

What belongs to an author but is used more by her readers?

her name

What do award-winning authors eat for breakfast?

"New-berry" pancakes

What do mystery writers use to hold their pants up?

"suspensers"

How did the pretzel maker end his mystery?

with a "twist"

How are mystery authors like Santa's elves before Christmas?

They "wrap" everything up.

What helps authors cool off on hot summer days?

reading "fan" mail

What happened when the surgeon wrote a very funny book?

It kept readers in "stitches."

Why did the actor get annoyed with the playwright?

She put words in his mouth.

Individual Authors

Who writes and illustrates children's books in his cellar?

Graeme "Base-ment"

Who's the gardener's favorite author?

Judy "Bloom"

What author makes good sandwiches?

Jan "Bread"

What would you get if you crossed a novel with Arthur and D. W.'s creator?

a "book-Marc"

What author enjoys kicking footballs?

Eve "Punting"

What author loves shopping?

Betsy "Buy-ers"

Why does music fill the library at Christmastime?

Lewis "Carrolls"

What would you get if you crossed the author of [name a Roald Dahl book] with Raggedy Ann?

Roald "Doll"

What boxer writes and illustrates children's books?

Tomie "de-POW-la"

What pig writes award-winning books for children?

Virginia "Ham-ilton"

What children's book authors like working in gardens?

Lillian, Russell, and Tana "Hoe-ban"

What duck wrote picture books about a nice teacher who sometimes pretends to be a mean teacher?

Harry "Mallard"

Who wrote and illustrated children's books when he wasn't keeping law and order in the Old West?

James "Marshal"

Why did Peggy Parish take a dictionary to the park?

She liked playing with words.

Where does Junie B. Jones go to play on the swings?

Barbara "Park"

What would you get if you crossed an author of funny books with an aspirin?

Dav "Pill-key"

What would you call clay dishes decorated with pictures of Jemima Puddleduck, Peter Rabbit, and Squirrel Nutkin?

Beatrix "Potter-y"

What author makes good sandwiches?

Cynthia "Rye-lant"

What would you get if you crossed the author of [name a Seuss book] with a Greek god?

Dr. "Zeus"

What author stole the plots for *Dr. Jekyll and Mr. Hyde*, *Kidnapped*, and *Treasure Island*?

"Robber" Louis Stevenson

Who writes children's books and makes men's clothing?

Theodore "Tailor"

What mountain lion wrote books about her pioneer family?

Laura Ingalls "Wildcat"

BOOKS

In General

What book should you always take when you camp?

a "book" of matches

When is a green book not a green book?

when it's "read" (red)

How do you make a bookend?

Read the last page.

What do library books wear when it's chilly?

dust "jackets"

What did the alien say to the library book?

"Take me to your 'reader.'"

What do you call stories about kittens?

"cat-tales"

What do you call stories about hogs?

"pig-tales"

What do you call stories about horses?

"pony-tales"

What do you call stories about patchwork quilts?

"scrap-books"

What do you call stories about skyscrapers?

"tall tales"

What would you call novels someone put in the oven?

"cooked-books"

Why did the silly kid put the book in the oven?

The cover said "Cook Book."

Why is reading cookbooks exciting?

They're "stirring."

What will you get if a spider makes its home in your library book?

"web pages"

Why did the silly kid put a ruler on the library book?

to get the story "straight"

Why didn't the monster finish the 300-page book?

He was full.

Why was the ending of *The Mummy Mystery* disappointing?

It didn't "wrap things up."

What would you get if you crossed [name a book] with a gymnast?

a book that flips its own pages

Why didn't the tree get much out of the book?

It just "leafed" through the pages.

How can you get a book to come to the phone?

"Page" it.

Why didn't the student believe what she read in the book about aquariums?

It sounded "fishy."

Why can't most readers understand the book about how birds fly?

It's over their heads.

Why can't most readers understand the book about rocks?

It's a "hard" subject.

Autobiographies

What did the car call the story of its life?

My "Auto-biography"

What does the critic think is wrong with the jogger's autobiography?

"run-on" sentences

What does the critic think is wrong with the judge's autobiography?

The "sentences" are too long.

What did the critic say about the skunk's auto-biography?

"It stinks."

Book Care

See also the book-care bookmarks in appendix C.

Why are library books like boomerangs?

They should always come back.

Why did the girl wrap the book about parrots in plastic bags before returning it to the library on a rainy day?

to keep it "Polly-unsaturated"

Why shouldn't you leave library books on the ground overnight?

In the morning they'll be "over dew" (overdue).

Why was Rip Van Winkle scared of going to the library after his twenty-year nap?

His books were way overdue.

Why couldn't King Arthur find his page?

He hadn't used a bookmark.

What would you get if you crossed something that keeps your place when you read with Arthur and D. W.'s creator?

a "book-Marc"

Book Reviews

What do you call it when critics express opinions about what they read through songs, dances, and skits?

a book "revue"

Why did the student think the book about boxing was amazing?

It "knocked him out!"

Why is the story about the cemetery confusing?

It has too many "plots."

Why do reviewers criticize the story about the dog that ran three miles to return a stick?

It's "far-fetched."

Why shouldn't you believe what you read in the book about garbage?

It's "rubbish."

Why did the reader think the book on hurricanes was amazing?

It "blew her away!"

Why do people get bored when they read *The Unsharpened Knife*?

It's very "dull."

Why does the critic highly recommend the book about lions and tigers?

She's "wild" about it.

What happens when people read the funny story about onions?

They laugh till they cry.

Why do readers laugh when they read the story about owls?

It's a "hoot."

What did critics do when they disliked the book about pizza?

They "panned" it.

Why do readers finish the book about Scotch tape in one sitting?

They can't "tear themselves away."

Parts of a Book

Why did the surgeon cut out the last few pages of his medical textbook?

to remove its "appendix"

What holds together the pages of a wizard's book?

"spell-binding"

Where do books sleep?

between "covers"

What comes at the beginning of a book about ghosts?

the "dead-ication"

What keeps library books warm when the weather gets chilly?

dust "jackets"

How did [name a fictional duck] start his/her autobiography?

with an "intro-duck-tion"

What do you call a company that prints nothing but dog books?

a "pup-lisher"

What did the carpenter make for the textbook?

a "table" of contents

What comes at the beginning of geography books?

a table of "continents"

Reference Books

Why can't you take out a reference book?

It already has a date.

ATLAS

What would you get if you crossed a runner with an atlas?

a "jog-raphy" book

Why will the librarian shelve the book with legends in the 900s instead of under 398.2?

It's an atlas.

How is an atlas like a book of folklore?

It has "legends."

What would you call a book of maps that show where lions and tigers live?

a "cat-las"

What would you call a very, very thick book of maps?

a "fat-las"

Create new riddles using words that rhyme with "at."

DICTIONARY

Where can you always find money when you're broke?

in the dictionary

Where does Christmas come before Valentine's Day?

in the dictionary

Create new variations of this.

Why does the witch [or Harry Potter] carry around a dictionary?

It helps her [him] "spell."

What happened when the meteorologist put her dictionary in the freezer?

She predicted a cold "spell."

What should you do if your dog eats your dictionary?

Take the words right out of its mouth.

Why do you need a dictionary to talk to giants?

They use "big words."

What would you get if you crossed an elephant with a dictionary?

"big words"

What would you get if you crossed a dictionary with a stinging insect?

a spelling bee

What would you get if you crossed a bookworm with a dictionary?

an animal that eats its words

What word does every dictionary spell wrong?

the word "wrong"

Why did the author take the dictionary to the park?

She liked playing with words.

What did one dictionary say to the other dictionary?

"I'd like a word with you."

What's happened ever since somebody stole our library's dictionary?

We're at a loss for words.

ENCYCLOPEDIA

What do you call someone who carries an encyclopedia in her pocket?

"smarty-pants"

What set of reference books helped the chicken start writing its report for school?

the "hen-cyclopedia"

What would you get if you crossed a set of reference books with a bike?

an "en-cycle-lopedia"

THESAURUS

What dinosaur knew many synonyms?

"Thesaurus" rex

What's a synonym?

the word you use when you can't spell the other one

COMPUTER SEARCHES

What has six legs and wings, flies, and knows its way around the Internet?

a computer "bug"

What's the most popular place for surfing?

the Internet

What did the computer do at the beach?

It "surfed" the Net.

What does a skunk use for surfing the Internet?

a "com-pew-ter"

How can you learn about hotels and motels before your vacation?

Search the "Inn-ternet."

How do sharks get information?

They search the "Fin-ternet."

How do snowmen find information?

They search the "Winter-net."

How can you learn to remove slivers from your fingers?

Search the "Splinter-net."

Create new riddles using words that rhyme with "Inter."

What do lumberjacks do before surfing the Net?

"log" on

What computer browser do witches use?

Internet "Hex-plorer"

What search engine do owls use?

"Ya-whoooo!"

Why don't fish look up information on the computer?

They're afraid of the "Net."

Why don't flies look up information on the computer?

They're afraid of the "Web."

Why did the police give the computer a ticket?

for speeding on the information highway

See also The Little Engine That Could *in chapter 8.*

ILLUSTRATORS

What did the illustrator call her first [or preliminary] drawings for a dog story?

"ruff" sketches

What would you get if you crossed an artist with Benedict Arnold?

an "illus-traitor"

What did the illustrators name their son?

Drew

Where do award-winning illustrators sleep?

on "Calde-cots"

How is Martin Handford like a rock concert?

He "draws" crowds.

How are the illustrations in [name any book illustrated by James Marshall] like karate?

They're "Marshall" art.

LIBRARIES

In General

What's the tallest building in town?

The library has the most "stories."

What does a fish use for borrowing books?

its library "cod"

What provides you with hours of entertainment and information, helps you keep up with current events, and is small enough to fit in your wallet?

a library card

Why does the girl borrow books about fishing every time she visits the library?

She's "hooked" on them.

What do librarians use for bait when they fish?

"book-worms"

What would you get if you crossed a librarian with a car?

a "bookmobile"

Why do the library's history books go out all the time?

They have many "dates."

What can you do in the library on the savannah?

Read between the "lions."

How did the librarian know who stole *The Scarlet Letter*?

He caught the thief red-handed.

Why doesn't anyone ever check out the library's copy of *Invisible Stanley*?

No one can see it.

See also "Why Should You Go to the Library?" and the reproducible library riddles for puppets in appendix C.

Library Manners

Why shouldn't you whisper to friends when the librarian reads your class a story?

It's not "aloud" (allowed).

What shouldn't you wear when you go to the library?

"loud" socks

What did the librarian tell the duck that raised its feathers noisily?

"Quiet, 'down.'"

What can you break in the library just by saying its name?

silence

Why are bowling alleys even quieter than libraries?

You can hear a "pin" drop.

Why did the tennis players get in trouble at the library?

They raised a "racket."

Why did [name a fictional horse] get in trouble at the library?

He/she was horsing around.

What did the librarian ask the students who carelessly put away books upside down, backward, and lying on top of each other?

"Aren't you ashamed of 'your-shelves'?"

Why did the boxer get in trouble at the library?

He "hit" the books.

Why did Curious George get in trouble at the library?

He "monkeyed" around with the books.

MAGAZINES

What does George Selden's Chester like to read every month?

Cricket magazine

What magazine keeps tumbling off library shelves?

Jack and Jill

What magazine does Wodney Wat read every month?

"Wanger Wick"

What magazine do gardeners read every month?

"Weeder's" Digest

What does E. B. White's Charlotte like to read every month?

Spider magazine

What magazine do toads like to read every month?

"Warts" Illustrated

What do clocks read every week?

Time magazine

NEWSPAPERS

What's black and white and "read" all over?

a newspaper

What do antelopes read every day?

the "gnus-paper"

What do cows read every day?

the "moos-paper"

What do amphibians read every day?

the "newts-paper"

Why did the newspaper reporter go to the ice-cream parlor?

to get the "scoop"

Why did the silly reporter write stories with peanut butter?

to "spread the word"

What did the silly reporter do when her editor asked her to cover a story?

She tucked her computer in bed.

Why should reporters take notes on a ruler when they interview people?

to keep their facts "straight"

What did the billionaire have when newspapers ran front-page stories about the fire at her mansion?

"flame" and fortune

What newspaper covered the story about Sleeping Beauty?

The Daily "Snooze"

What prints news about airports?

The "Fly-Paper"

What prints news about the beach?

The "Sand-Paper"

What part of the newspaper never has anything nice to say?

the "cross-word" puzzle

POETRY

Why do poets have trouble making a living?

Rhyme doesn't pay.

What turtle wrote funny poems for children?

"Shell" Silverstein

What did [name a children's poet] plant on Arbor Day?

a "poe-tree"

What do forest rangers read?

"poe-tree"

Why shouldn't you write poetry when you have a bad day?

You'd make things go from bad to "verse."

What do you call poems about outer space?

"uni-verse"

What do you call poems when you read them backward?

"re-verse"

What do you call funny five-line verses about trees?

"limb-ericks"

What would you call seventeen-syllable poems about doves?

"hai-coo"

READING

Why will reading ghost stories help you cool off on hot summer days?

They're "chilling."

Why can you always find plenty to read in a skyscraper?

    It has many "stories."

Why is a fly in the alphabet soup?

    It's learning to read.

Why do skeletons read riddle books?

    to tickle their funny bones

What would you call a cat that reads riddle books?

    a giggle puss

What would you hear if you read riddles to bananas?

    "peels" of laughter

Why did the teddy bear need mending after reading a riddle book?

    It split its sides laughing.

What happened when the statue read a riddle book?

    It "cracked a smile."

What happened when the duck read a riddle book?

    It "quacked" up.

What happened when the lion read a riddle book?

    It "roared" with laughter.

What happened when the wolf read a riddle book?

    It "howled" with laughter.

What did Mother Nature hear when she read riddles during a hurricane?

    "gales" of laughter

What happens when Mother Nature reads a really funny book?

    The wind "howls."

What happens when Mother Nature reads a really sad book?

    The wind "wails."

What happened when Frankenstein's monster read a riddle book?

    It laughed its head off.

What happened when Frankenstein's monster read a really sad story?

    It cried its eyes out.

Why do astronauts read a lot on space missions?

    They can't put their books down.

Why do kittens read adventure stories?

    They love a good "yarn."

What do frogs like best about fairy tales?

    the "hoppy" endings

Why do lions eat raw meat?

    They can't read cookbooks.

What do bakers read to their children at night?

    "bread-time" stories

What do astronauts like to read?

    "comet" books

What do bank robbers like to read?

    "crook-books"

What do musicians like to read?

    "note-books"

What do pythons like to read?

"gripping" tales

See also riddles under "Books"—"In General" and adapt where possible. For example, ask "What do hogs like to read? 'pig-tales.'" See also the reproducible library riddles for puppets in appendix C. Ask "What do _____ like to read?" instead of "What do _____ borrow from the library?"

8 Laughing at "Our-shelves"
Riddles about Specific Books

For any book, substitute the name of its writer or artist for "author" and "illustrator." See also chapters with riddles related to a title's subject. For example, check chapter 10 for animal books. See also riddles under "Authors" and "Illustrators" in chapter 7.

ANY BOOK ABOUT AN INVISIBLE CHARACTER

Fill in the name of any invisible character.

Why did _____ get terrible grades?
   His/her teacher kept marking him/her absent.

What did the nurse say when _____ went in for a checkup?
   "The doctor can't see you right now."

Why won't _____ be able to fool you?
   You can see right through him/her.

Why did _____ look in the mirror?
   to see if he/she still wasn't there

Who always wins at hide-and-seek?
   _____

Why doesn't anyone ever check out the library's copy of _____?
   No one can see it.

ANY BOOK THAT'S ALSO A MOVIE

What did the goat say when it ate the DVD of [name a book that's also a movie]?
   "I liked the book better."

ANY GIANT STORY

Fill in the name of any fictional giant.

What would happen if _____ trampled your vegetable garden?
   You'd have "squash."

What would you have if _____ tramped across your potato field?
   "smashed" potatoes

See also "Wild Animals"—"Elephants" in chapter 10. Substitute "giant" for "elephant" when "big" is in the answer.

ANY SPY STORY

Fill in the name of any spy, or use "secret agent."

What does _____ like to drink in the fall?

   apple "spy-der"

What would you call _____ if he/she spilled ice cream in his/her lap?

   "spy" à la mode

What kind of pet snake would _____ like to have?

   a "spy-thon"

Where does _____ buy groceries?

   the "snooper-market"

Why did _____ hire an exterminator?

   His/her room was "bugged."

DR. SEUSS BOOKS

What would you call a play that combined Dr. Seuss's stories with Shakespeare?

   Green Eggs and "Ham-let"

What would you get if you crossed the author of [name a Seuss book] with a Greek god?

   Dr. "Zeus"

See also chapter 7, substituting "Dr. Seuss" for "author" and "illustrator." For his birthday, on March 2, adapt riddles from chapter 11.

Riddles for Unusual Dr. Seuss Creatures

Fill in the name of any Dr. Seuss creature.

How long should the legs of a _____ be?

   long enough to reach the ground

Where can you find a _____?

   That depends on where you left it.

What looks most like a _____?

   another _____

See also "Any Animal" in chapter 10.

And to Think That I Saw It on Mulberry Street

What would Marco call a procession of cats marching down Mulberry Street?

   a "purr-ade"

Bartholomew and the Oobleck

How could Bartholomew tell that the oobleck was clumsy?

   It kept falling.

What did King Derwin get when the royal servants forgot to clean his telescope?

   a "dirty look"

Why did King Derwin have a royal seal?

   Royal walruses eat too much!

The Cat in the Hat

What would you call kittens wearing the same tall, floppy, red-and-white-striped hat?

   "Copy-cats" in the Hat

What's black and white and red all over?

the Cat in the Hat with a sunburn

What would you get if you crossed what the Cat in the Hat carries with Horton?

an "umbrella-phant"

Why does the Cat in the Hat eat meals on top of the ball?

to "balance" his diet

The Five Hundred Hats of Bartholomew Cubbins

Who makes King Derwin remove his crown?

the royal barber

What did King Derwin get from his dentist?

a new "crown"

Fox in Socks

Why does the fox wear red socks?

His blue ones are in the wash.

Green Eggs and Ham

What would you get if you crossed a frog with a pet rodent?

"green legs and ham-ster"

What will the narrator of *Green Eggs and Ham* never eat for breakfast?

his lunch and supper

What would happen if Sam-I-Am dropped his green eggs and ham in the water?

They'd get wet.

Why didn't Sam-I-Am tell jokes to the green eggs?

He feared they'd crack up.

Horton Hatches the Egg

Why did Horton sit on the ax?

to "hatch-et"

Why did Mayzie fly off to Palm Beach?

It was too far to walk.

How was Horton's promise like Mayzie's egg?

He tried not to break it.

What could seasick Horton have said to stop the ship?

"'Whoa, whoa, whoa' the boat."

What did Horton do when it poured and it lightninged?

He got wet.

Horton Hears a Who!

How did the sour kangaroo feel when Horton talked to the dust speck?

"hopping mad"

What's the tallest building in *Who*-ville?

The library has the most stories.

Which *Who* can jump higher than the Eiffelberg Tower?

They all can. The Eiffelberg Tower can't jump.

What makes more of a racket than a *Who* beating on an old cranberry can?

ten *Whos* beating on ten old cranberry cans

How the Grinch Stole Christmas!

What's wiggly, has no legs, and tried to steal Christmas?

a "Grinch-worm"

Why did the Grinch feel sick while sliding down the *Whos'* chimney with empty bags in his fist?

He was coming down with something.

How do the little *Who* stockings celebrate Christmas?

They "hang around."

What would you call JoJo's tricycle if he rode it very, very fast?

a "tot" rod

Why did the Grinch send Cindy-Lou *Who* to bed?

The bed wouldn't come to her.

The Lorax

What kind of ax can't you use to cut trees?

the "Lor-ax"

How did the Truffula Tree feel when the Once-ler didn't chop it down?

"re-leafed"

Why couldn't the Truffula Tree answer the Once-ler's question?

He'd "stumped" it.

McElligot's Pool

Where is McElligot's Pool deepest?

at the bottom

How did Marco communicate with the fish in McElligot's Pool?

He dropped them a "line."

What did Marco catch when he went ice fishing in McElligot's Pool?

a cold

What was Marco trying to catch when he used peanut butter for bait?

"jelly-fish"

Why does Marco keep fishing in McElligot's Pool?

He's "hooked."

Oh, the Places You'll Go!

Why should you take a cow with you when you get on your way?

to "moooo-ve" mountains

What will walk ahead of you in the morning and behind you in the afternoon as you go on your way?

your shadow

What did the stringed instrument say to the person playing it in the Bright Places?

"Quit picking on me."

The Sneetches and Other Stories

How did the Sneetches' beaches greet the tide when it came in?

"Long time, no 'sea.'"

How did the Sneetches' beaches say good-bye to the tide?

"'Sea' you later."

What did the highway built around the Zax say to the jackhammer?

"You 'crack me up'!"

What belongs to all twenty-three Daves but is used more by Mrs. McCave?

their name

Why were the pale green pants lonely?

> They had "no body" (nobody) to play with.

What would you get if you crossed the Brickel bush with a Stickle-Bush Tree from *If I Ran the Circus*?

> sore hands

Thidwick, the Big-Hearted Moose

Why did Thidwick's antlers think Uncle Woodpecker was dull?

> He "bored" them.

When does Thidwick lose his antlers?

> in the fall

Why won't the pests eat dessert at the Harvard Club?

> They're "stuffed."

Yertle the Turtle and Other Stories

What would you get if you crossed Yertle the Turtle with a children's poet?

> "Shell" Silverstein

Why didn't Yertle pull his head in his shell?

> He had claustrophobia.

What would you get if you crossed a fictional girl detective with Gertrude's tail?

> Nancy "Droop"

Where could Gertrude McFuzz get back her old tail?

> a "re-tail" store

How is the rabbit like a potato?

> It keeps its eyes "peeled."

What does the bear like to read?

> best "smellers"

EASIES

Agent A to Agent Z, by Andy Rash

Who follows a secret agent around?

> a secret "B-gent"

What has no legs, slithers on the ground, and wears a trench coat?

> a "spy-thon"

See also "Any Spy Story."

Alexander and the Terrible, Horrible, No Good, Very Bad Day, by Judith Viorst

What happened when Alexander wrote a poem about his terrible, horrible, no good, very bad day?

> He made things go from bad to "verse."

Why did Alexander's shoe have a terrible, horrible, no good, very bad day?

> It started off on the wrong foot.

And the Dish Ran Away with the Spoon, by Janet Stevens and Susan Stevens Crummel

Why does Dish need to ask Spoon for a loan?

> It's "broke."

See also reproducible Mother Goose riddles for dish puppets in appendix C.

Arthur Series, by Lillian Hoban

What did Lillian Hoban's Arthur grow in his flower garden?

> "chimp-pansies"

What would you call Lillian Hoban's Arthur when he's taking PE?

a "gym-panzee"

What kind of cookie does Lillian Hoban's Arthur like best?

chocolate "chimp"

Arthur's Chicken Pox, by Marc Brown

What did Marc Brown use for writing the rough draft of *Arthur's Chicken Pox*?

"scratch" paper

Berenstain Bears Series, by Stan Berenstain and Jan Berenstain

See the book-care bookmarks in appendix C.

Caps for Sale, by Esphyr Slobodkina

What would you call a book that combined *Stellaluna* and *Caps for Sale*?

The Bat in the Hat

A Chair for My Mother, by Vera Williams

What kind of furniture wears bracelets?

"arm-chairs"

Chrysanthemum, by Kevin Henkes

What belongs to Chrysanthemum but is used more by her classmates and teacher?

her name

Cloudy with a Chance of Meatballs, by Judi Barrett

What formed on Chewandswallow's streets the day it rained potatoes?

"spud-dles"

Corduroy, by Don Freeman

What picture book character does Corduroy look for when he visits the library?

Oliver Button

Why did Lisa have to mend Corduroy after reading him a riddle book?

He split his sides laughing.

Curious George Series, by H. A. Rey and Margret Rey

What storybook monkey throws temper tantrums?

"Furious" George

What would Curious George become if he ate too much ice cream?

a "chunky monkey"

What does Curious George use to get into his house?

a "mon-key"

What would Curious George get if he opened his own store?

"monkey business"

What did Curious George use to fix the sink?

a "monkey wrench"

What does Curious George play on when he goes to the park?

the "monkey bars"

Why did Curious George get in trouble at the library?

He "monkeyed" around with the books.

Dog Breath! The Horrible Trouble with Hally Tosis, by Dav Pilkey

Why did the burglars take a bath before sneaking into the Tosis house?

>to make a "clean getaway"

See also "Wild Animals"—"Skunks" in chapter 10. Substitute "Hally Tosis" for "skunk" where appropriate.

Duck for President, by Doreen Cronin

Did Duck run for reelection?

>No, he stepped "down."

Eloise Series, by Hilary Knight

Where does Santa deliver Eloise's presents?

>The Plaza "Ho-Ho-Hotel"

"The Farmer in the Dell" (Any Version)

Who drives a tractor and makes great corned beef sandwiches?

>The Farmer in the "Deli"

Fluffy Series, by Kate McMullan

What did Ms. Day's students call Fluffy when he got greedy?

>a "gimme" pig

Frances Series, by Russell Hoban

How does Russell Hoban's Frances try to get her own way?

>She "badgers" people.

Frog and Toad Series, by Arnold Lobel

What do Frog and Toad play when they're tired?

>"sleep-frog"

What would you get if you crossed Arnold Lobel's Frog with Lynne Reid Banks's Houdini (or Betty G. Birney's Humphrey)?

>"green legs and ham-ster"

Ginger Jumps, by Lisa Campbell Ernst

What did Ginger do when she went to a basketball game?

>She jumped through the hoops.

See also "Circuses" in chapter 16.

Goodnight Moon, by Margaret Wise Brown

What was the little calf's favorite bedtime story?

>*Goodnight "Moooo-n"*

Gregory, the Terrible Eater, by Mitchell Sharmat

What does Gregory eat for breakfast?

>"goat-meal"

What did Gregory get when he ate a key ring?

>lockjaw

What did Gregory get when he ate a window?

>stomach "panes"

See also "Any Book That's Also a Movie."

Harry the Dirty Dog, by Gene Zion

What did Harry become when he took a bath with a mouse?

"squeaky" clean

Harry's Dog, by Barbara Ann Porte

What kind of dog won't make Harry's father sneeze?

a hot dog

The Hat, by Jan Brett

What would you call a book that combined *Stellaluna* with *The Hat*?

The Bat in the Hat

Henry and Mudge Series, by Cynthia Rylant

What should Henry give Mudge when he has a fever?

Mustard's always good for a hot dog.

See also the book-care bookmarks in appendix C.

Hooway for Wodney Wat, by Helen Lester

When did Wodney Wat say "whoa" to his horse?

at the end of their "wide"

What magazine does Wodney Wat read every month?

"Wanger Wick"

How can Wodney Wat say "Richard and Robert have a Labrador retriever" without any *r*'s?

"Dick and Bob have a dog."

What did Wodney Wat put on top of the house he built for his dog?

a "woof"

Hot-Air Henry, by Mary Calhoun

Why won't Mary Calhoun's Henry take advice from the balloon?

It's full of hot air.

What would you call Mary Calhoun's Henry if he fussed about finishing last in a balloon race?

a "soar" loser

Hot Fudge, by James Howe

What would you call Cynthia Rylant's dog books if Toby accidentally smeared chocolate on them?

Henry and "Smudge"

"I Know an Old Lady Who Swallowed a Fly" (Any Version)

Why did the old lady swallow a fly?

She had a "frog" in her throat.

Imogene's Antlers, by David Small

Why did Imogene grow antlers?

She put too much "moose" in her hair.

"The Itsy Bitsy Spider" (Any Version)

What scatterbrained creature climbed up the waterspout?

the itsy, "ditzy" spider

Kat Kong, by Dav Pilkey

Why did Kat Kong climb to the top of the Romano Inn?

He didn't fit in the elevator.

The Little Engine That Could, by Watty Piper

What would you call the Little Engine That Could if she carried gum?

a "chew-chew" train

What storybook character said, "I think I can find it. I think I can find it. I think I can find it"?

The Little "Search Engine" That Could

What engine would never be able to pull the little train up the mountain?

a "search engine"

Madeline Series, by Ludwig Bemelmans

Why did Miss Clavel take her book to the middle of the girls' room?

to "read between the lines"

What kind of dancing does Madeline like?

line dancing

What sport is just right for Madeline and her friends?

in-line skating

Martha Series, by Susan Meddaugh

Why is a fly in Martha's alphabet soup?

It's learning to read.

What's more amazing than a dog that can talk?

a spelling bee

How did Helen get Martha into the shoe store that didn't allow dogs?

She had to "sneak-'er" in.

Why did the workers lose their jobs at Granny's Soup Company?

They got "canned."

Mike Mulligan and His Steam Shovel, by Virginia Lee Burton

What did Mike Mulligan call Mary Anne when she got angry?

a "steamed-shovel"

Mirette on the High Wire, by Emily Arnold McCully

What did Mirette say to the tightrope?

"'Hi, wire.'"

See also "Circuses" in chapter 16.

The Mixed-Up Chameleon, by Eric Carle

What would you get if you crossed [name any fictional horse] with Eric Carle's mixed-up chameleon?

a horse of a different color

Officer Buckle and Gloria, by Peggy Rathmann

What storybook character helps you fasten your belt?

Officer Buckle

What does Officer Buckle call Gloria when she's sick?

a "germy" shepherd

Oliver Button Is a Sissy, by Tomie dePaola

What picture book character does Corduroy look for when he visits the library?

Oliver Button

What does Oliver Button drink?

"tap" water

How did Oliver Button get wet when he tap danced?

He fell in the sink.

The Polar Express, by Chris Van Allsburg

What train takes children to the dentist's office on Christmas Eve?

The "Molar" Express

Rabbit-cadabra! by James Howe

What did The Amazing Karlovsky perform after eating the breakfast cereal that's just for kids?

magic "Trix"

Sheila Rae, the Brave, by Kevin Henkes

What will Sheila Rae, the Brave, never eat with her soup?

a "chicken" sandwich

Why didn't Sheila Rae, the Brave, cross the road?

She wasn't a "chicken."

Shrek, by William Steig

What storybook ogre keeps biting his nails?

a nervous "Shrek"

Sir Small and the Dragonfly, by Jane O'Connor

What insects fought knights in the Middle Ages?

"dragon-flies"

Skyfire, by Frank Asch

What will Bear find at the end of every rainbow?

the letter "w"

Stellaluna, by Janell Cannon

Why does the reader highly recommend Stellaluna?

He's "batty" about it.

What would you call a book that combined Stellaluna with Caps for Sale?

The Bat in the Hat

What would Stellaluna become if she took gymnastics lessons?

an "acro-bat"

The Stinky Cheese Man and Other Fairly Stupid Tales, by Jon Scieszka

How could the Stinky Cheese Man have defended himself from the fox?

with kung "phew!"

See also "Wild Animals"—"Skunks" in chapter 10. Substitute "Stinky Cheese Man" for "skunk" where appropriate.

The Story of Ferdinand, by Munro Leaf

What chain of bookstores doesn't sell Munro Leaf's The Story of Ferdinand?

Barnes and "No-bull" (Noble)

What would you call Munro Leaf's Ferdinand when he's taking a nap?

a "bull-dozer"

How did Munro Leaf's Ferdinand get hurt at the archery contest?

> Somebody hit the "bull's eye."

Sylvester and the Magic Pebble, by William Steig

What did guests play at Sylvester's birthday party?

> "Pin the Tail on the Host"

What would you get if you crossed William Steig's Sylvester with an insect?

> a "braying" mantis

What do Sylvester and his parents use to open their front door?

> a "don-key"

The Tale of Peter Rabbit, by Beatrix Potter

Who gave parking tickets to Flopsy, Mopsy, and Cotton-tail?

> "Meter" Rabbit

Who always peeks when playing hide-and-seek with Flopsy, Mopsy, and Cotton-tail?

> "Cheater" Rabbit

Who snatches toys away from Flopsy, Mopsy, and Cotton-tail?

> Peter "Grab-it"

What do you call stories about Peter Rabbit's brother?

> "Cotton-tales"

Walter's Tail, by Lisa Campbell Ernst

Why does Walter wag his tail?

> No one will wag it for him.

How are authors of heartwarming stories like Lisa Campbell Ernst's Walter?

> Their "tales" are "moving."

The Wolf's Chicken Stew, by Keiko Kasza

What did the wolf do when the family of chickens moved in next door?

> had his neighbors for supper

What shouldn't Mr. Wolf eat when he needs to feel brave?

> "chicken" stew

FAIRY TALES AND FOLKTALES

In General

What do frogs like best about fairy tales?

> the "hoppy" endings

Who never smiled or laughed while collecting fairy tales?

> the "Grim" brothers

What do you call stories where good guys lose and bad guys live happily ever after?

> "unfair-y" tales

Abiyoyo, by Pete Seeger

What was the favorite toy of Pete Seeger's dancing giant?

> his "Abi-yo-yo"

Anansi and the Talking Melon, by Eric A. Kimmel

What's more amazing than a talking melon?

> a spelling bee

"The Arabian Nights"

Why does Scheherazade deserve a raise at the bank?

She's a great "teller."

Why did the magic lamp get angry with Aladdin?

He rubbed it the wrong way.

What did the magic lamp give Aladdin when he wrapped a scarf around it?

"warm wishes"

What did Aladdin's lamp give the basketball player?

three "swishes"

What did Aladdin's lamp give the beaver?

"tree" wishes

How did Dr. Aladdin cure patients with his magic lamp?

He wished them well.

"Beauty and the Beast"

What fairy tale is about a beautiful snob and an ugly monster?

"'Snooty' and the Beast"

What did Beauty break in the castle without even touching it?

the witch's spell

"Chicken Little"

What did Foxy Loxy say to Chicken Little and her friends?

"It's a pleasure to 'eat' you."

"Cinderella"

Why does spending nights in the fireplace make Cinderella feel rested?

She "sleeps like a log."

What's big and gray and wears glass slippers?

"Cinderella-phant"

What size is Cinderella's slipper?

one foot long

What did Cinderella wear at bedtime?

glass bunny slippers

What did Cinderella wear when she went to the beach?

glass "flippers"

Why wasn't the prince allowed to pitch for Cinderella's baseball team?

He threw too many "balls."

See also "Any Sport" in chapter 14.

"The Emperor's New Clothes"

What did the antelope emperor want?

"gnu" clothes

What did the maid call the palace windows when she had to wash them all?

royal "panes"

Fin M'Coul, by Tomie dePaola

What would you get if you crossed an Irish giant with an ice cube?

Fin "M'Cool"

"The Fisherman and His Wife"

How did the fisherman keep in touch with the magic fish?

He dropped it a "line."

"The Frog Prince"

What kind of candy turns frogs into princes?

Hershey's Kisses

What time was it when the witch turned the prince into a frog?

"spring-time"

What happened after the Frog Prince married the princess?

They lived "hoppily" ever after.

See also "Wild Animals"—"Frogs and Toads" in chapter 10.

"The Gingerbread Man"

What did the gingerbread man get from his eye doctor?

contact raisins

What did the gingerbread man need after twisting his ankle?

a candy "cane"

What does the gingerbread man put on his bed?

cookie "sheets"

Why did the gingerbread man go to the doctor?

He felt "crumb-y."

"Goldilocks and the Three Bears"

What fairy-tale character is never warm?

"Cold-ilocks"

What did the three bears put on their door to keep out unwanted guests?

"Goldi-locks"

What do the three bears put on bagels?

"Goldi-lox"

What did the three bears eat when they ran out of money?

"poor-ridge"

Why didn't Mama want to eat cold porridge?

She couldn't "bear" it.

"Hansel and Gretel"

What was the saddest candy in the witch's gingerbread house?

the "glum-drops"

What did the witch use for making Hansel's cage?

chocolate "bars"

Where did Hansel and Gretel's witch sleep?

her "ginger-bed"

Why did Hansel and Gretel's witch need to move?

They ate her out of house and home.

How are Hansel and Gretel doing after surgery?

They're not "out of the woods" yet.

Itching and Twitching, by Patricia C. McKissack

Why do monkeys always scratch themselves?

No one else knows where they itch.

"Jack and the Beanstalk"

What fairy tale tells about a boy who chats with vegetables?

> "Jack and the 'Beans Talk'"

What did Jack get when he planted his Easter candy?

> a "jellybean-stalk"

What bunny climbed a giant beanstalk?

> a "Jack-rabbit"

What grew on Jack's beanstalk?

> "climb-a" beans

Why did Jack climb the beanstalk?

> It didn't have an elevator.

How did the giant find out about his surprise birthday party?

> Jack "spilled the beans."

See also "Any Giant Story."

Jamie O'Rourke and the Big Potato, by Tomie dePaola

What did Jamie O'Rourke do when he got a job in a bakery?

> "loafed" around

King Arthur (Any Version)

Where could King Arthur buy an animal with two humps?

> a "camel lot"

What did King Arthur call his sword when it got frozen in a block of ice?

> "Excali-brrrr"

What was baby Lancelot before he learned to walk?

> a "knight" crawler

What made Sir Lancelot tired every morning?

> working the "knight" shift

What made Sir Lancelot wake up screaming?

> "knight-mares"

Create new riddles substituting "knight" for "night."

"The Little Red Hen"

How is an embarrassed chicken like the fairy-tale character who did things herself?

> She's a little "red" hen.

Why did it take the Little Red Hen a long time to make bread?

> She started from "scratch."

Why did the banker help the Little Red Hen make bread?

> She liked working with "dough."

"Little Red Riding Hood"

Why did Little Red Riding Hood take a basket of goodies to her grandmother?

> The basket wouldn't take itself.

Who wears a red cloak, takes goodies to her grandmother, and makes rules that all have to obey?

> Little Red Riding "Should"

Who wears a red cloak, takes goodies to her grandmother, and got into a car accident?

> Little "Wreck" Riding Hood

"Paul Bunyan"

Who's extremely tall, cuts down trees, and has sore feet?

Paul "Bunion"

What would you get if you crossed Sleeping Beauty with Paul Bunyan?

a "slumber-jack"

What does Paul Bunyan do with his blue ox, Babe?

He tries to cheer her up.

"The Pied Piper of Hamelin"

What did the Pied Piper say when he lost his flute?

"Oh, rats!"

What happened when the Pied Piper ate lemons?

He played "sour" notes.

"The Princess and the Pea"

What letter of the alphabet kept a princess awake all night?

a "p"

What fairy tale tells about a royal girl and the noisy chickens that kept her awake?

"The Princess and the 'Peeps'"

How did the princess feel when she couldn't fall asleep?

"pea-ved"

"Puss in Boots"

What baby kitten helped the miller's son marry the king's daughter?

Puss in "Booties"

What story tells about a pirate cat and its treasure?

"Puss 'n' 'Booty'"

What storybook cat played a trumpet?

Puss 'n' "Toots"

"Rapunzel"

What fairy-tale character liked playing with words?

"Ra-pun-zel"

What upsets Rapunzel more than anything else?

bad hair days

Why was Rapunzel annoyed with the prince?

He got in her hair.

Robin Hood (Any Version)

Why did Robin Hood rob the rich?

The poor had nothing to steal.

Who stole from the rich, gave to the poor, and made rules that all had to obey?

Robin "Should"

Was Robin Hood nervous about entering the archery contest in Nottingham?

No, but his arrows were all in a "quiver."

Who kept Sherwood Forest clean?

"Maid" Marian

Where did Robin Hood buy flowers for Maid Marian?

Sherwood "Florist"

"Rumpelstiltskin"

What fairy-tale character never irons his clothes?

"Rumpled-stiltskin"

Who has a funny name, spins straw into gold, and complains all the time?

"Grumble-stiltskin"

What did Rumpelstiltskin eat while turning straw into gold?

"spin-ach"

"The Shoemaker and the Elves"

What did the elves sing while making shoes?

"sole" music

"Sleeping Beauty"

What would you get if you crossed Sleeping Beauty with Paul Bunyan?

a "slumber-jack"

Who hosted the world's longest slumber party?

Sleeping Beauty

What fairy tale tells about a lovely princess who cleaned a castle for 100 years?

"'Sweeping' Beauty"

What fairy tale tells about a lovely frog that fell asleep for 100 years?

"'Leaping' Beauty"

Create new riddles using words that rhyme with "sleeping."

Why did Sleeping Beauty sleep for 100 years?

Her alarm clock was broken.

What made Sleeping Beauty wake up with chocolate smeared all over her mouth?

a Hershey's Kiss

"Snow White"

Who has dark hair and white skin, lives with seven little men, and weighs 300 pounds?

Snow "Wide"

What did Snow White say when she dropped off film to be developed?

"Someday my 'prints' will come."

Why do [name a sport] teams want Snow White to referee their games?

She's the "fairest" one of all.

What did the seven dwarfs' rake say to their hoe?

"Hi, 'hoe.'"

Strega Nona, by Tomie dePaola

What would you get if you crossed an Egyptian queen with Strega Nona's magic pot?

"Cleo-pasta"

"The Three Billy Goats Gruff"

Where did the troll make sketches?

under a "draw-bridge"

What bridge is too small for a troll to live under?

the "bridge" of your nose

Who threatened to knock the troll off the bridge but would never have hurt him?

the Big Billy Goat "Bluff"

What does the Big Billy Goat Gruff use for making sandwiches?

"troll" wheat bread

Why can't his brothers have a conversation when the Big Billy Goat Gruff is around?

He "butts" in.

"The Three Little Pigs"

What would you call the three little pigs if they'd built houses in the middle of a highway?

"road hogs"

Why did the three little pigs hire a maid?

Their house was a pigsty.

What did the first little pig say when he put the finishing touch on his house?

"That's the last straw."

What did the second little pig use to build a house by the river?

"fish-sticks"

What would you get if you crossed the third little pig with a hen?

a "brick-layer"

What did the third little pig call his high-rise apartment building?

a "sty-scraper"

How could the third little pig tell that the wolf was angry?

He left in a "huff."

"Tom Thumb"

How can the inch-high fairy-tale character tell when his watermelons are ripe?

Tom thumps.

How did the police know Tom Thumb stole the museum's valuable statue?

His "Thumb-prints" were on it.

"The Tortoise and the Hare"

What did the hare drink during the race with the tortoise?

"running" water

How can you get the lazy hare to finish the race with the tortoise?

Jump-start him.

What did the tortoise's opponent say after losing the race?

"I'm having a bad 'hare' day."

What would you call the hare after losing the race to the tortoise?

a "cross"-country runner

What race can neither the tortoise nor the hare ever win?

the "human race"

FICTION

The Adventures of Huckleberry Finn, by Mark Twain

What bedtime story should you read your pet fish?

The Adventures of Huckleberry "Fin"

The Adventures of Tom Sawyer, by Mark Twain

Where did Tom Sawyer and Becky Thatcher buy supplies to explore McDougal's cave?

"Cave-Mart"

Alice's Adventures in Wonderland, by Lewis Carroll

In what famous fantasy does a girl dream about visiting an unusual place where everyone makes mistakes?

Alice's Adventures in "Blunder-land"

Amelia Series, by Marissa Moss

What does Marissa Moss's Amelia use for writing stories about streams?

a "note-brook"

Anne of Green Gables, by L. M. Montgomery

What classic novel tells the story of an orphaned insect that went to live on a Canadian farm?

"Ant" of Green Gables

Babe and Me, by Dan Gutman

What legendary baseball slugger was still in diapers?

"Baby" Ruth

Babe: The Gallant Pig, by Dick King-Smith

What does Dick King-Smith's gallant pig have in common with a famous baseball slugger?

the first name Babe

What did Fly say to get the sheep's attention?

"Hey, 'ewe'!"

How did Babe fool the sheep?

He pulled the wool over their eyes.

See also Babe and Me.

Ben and Me, by Robert Lawson

What book did Robert Lawson write about a famous American visiting a butcher shop?

Ben and "Meat"

What book did Robert Lawson write about a famous American practicing scales in music class?

Ben and "Mi"

Charlie and the Chocolate Factory, by Roald Dahl

What tree owns a magical chocolate factory?

"Willow" Wonka

What kind of motorcycle does Willy Wonka ride?

a "Charlie-Davidson"

What did Violet chew when she was sad?

"bubble-glum"

Charlotte's Web, by E. B. White

Why was Wilbur grateful to Charlotte?

She'd "saved his bacon."

What does E. B. White's Charlotte like to read every month?

Spider magazine

Why won't Fern let Wilbur sleep with her?

He's a "bed hog."

Why were Fern and Wilbur suspicious when Templeton started using cologne?

They "smelled a rat."

What did Charlotte say when Wilbur told her he'd taken a bath?

"Hogwash!"

A Christmas Carol, by Charles Dickens

What would you get if you crossed a lobster with Ebenezer Scrooge?

a "shellfish" person

Why did Ebenezer Scrooge like finding coal in his stocking on Christmas morning?

It saved money on heat.

What did Ebenezer Scrooge wear when he played ice hockey?

"cheap-skates"

The Chronicles of Narnia, by C. S. Lewis

What do Narnia's residents wear over their pajamas?

"ward-robes"

Cracker Jackson, by Betsy Byars

What storybook character goes well with soup?

Cracker Jackson

What does Cracker Jackson's classmate chew?

"Bubba-gum"

The Cricket in Times Square, by George Selden

What does George Selden's Chester like to read every month?

Cricket magazine

Where did Chester Cricket learn how to multiply?

"Times-Table" Square

Doctor Dolittle Series, by Hugh Lofting

Who's so busy talking to animals that he rarely accomplishes anything?

Dr. "Do-Little"

Dr. Jekyll and Mr. Hyde, by Robert Louis Stevenson

What did Dr. Jekyll like to play?

"Hyde"-and-seek

Where does Dr. Jekyll go to get away from it all?

his "Hyde-away"

Dracula, by Bram Stoker

Who has Transylvania's most dangerous job?

Count Dracula's dentist

See also "Vampires" in chapter 12.

Flat Stanley, by Jeff Brown

What would happen if a piano fell on Jeff Brown's Stanley?

He would "B flat."

Frankenstein, by Mary Shelley

Why did Dr. Frankenstein stop feeling lonely?

He made new friends.

What does Dr. Frankenstein drive?

a "monster truck"

Where did Dr. Frankenstein get his monster a new hand?

a "second-hand" store

What did the monster do when Dr. Frankenstein asked for help?

gave him a hand

What did the monster do when Dr. Frankenstein wanted to talk about his troubles?

lent him its ear

Why was Frankenstein's monster missing a part of itself after music class?

It "sang its heart out."

See also "Reading" in chapter 7.

Goosebumps Series, by R. L. Stine

What would you call a book that combined nursery rhymes with R. L. Stine's scary stories?

Mother "Goose-bumps"

What does R. L. Stine have on the front and back of his car?

"Goosebump-ers"

Harry Potter Series, by J. K. Rowling

What do you call a man who makes clay dishes and never shaves?

"hairy" potter

Who is a student at Hogwarts, plays Quidditch, and turns into a werewolf when the moon is full?

"Hairy" Potter

Who goes to Hogwarts, plays Quidditch, and has long ears?

"Hare-y" Potter

Who has a magic wand, plays Quidditch, and lives in the sea?

Harry "Otter"

What's yellow with black stripes, makes honey, and goes to Hogwarts?

a "spelling" bee

Why does Harry Potter always carry a dictionary?

It helps him "spell."

What did Harry Potter get after riding the merry-go-round all day?

dizzy "spells"

What did Harry Potter do when he got tired of April showers?

He cast a dry "spell."

What did Harry Potter do when he got tired of the heat wave?

He cast a cold "spell."

Hatchet, by Gary Paulsen

Why did the chicken sit on Brian's ax?

to "hatch-et"

Why didn't the hatchet go to Brian's birthday party?

It wasn't "axed."

"The Headless Horseman"

See "The Legend of Sleepy Hollow."

Heidi, by Joanna Spyri

What game do children in the Swiss Alps play?

"Heidi"-and-seek

How to Eat Fried Worms, by Thomas Rockwell

What did Alan make Billy eat in the library?

a "book-worm"

The Hundred and One Dalmatians, by Dodie Smith

Why don't the hundred and one Dalmatians enjoy playing hide-and-seek?

They're always "spotted."

What did the woman who stole the Dalmatian puppies drink on hot summer days?

"Cruel-Aid"

Judy Moody Saves the World, by Megan McDonald

How did Judy Moody try to save the world?

She took her globe to the bank.

Junie B. Jones Series, by Barbara Park

Who stars in a funny series of books, has a baby brother named Ollie, and makes honey?

Junie "Bee" Jones

What did Junie B. Jones want to be when the bakers got married?

their "flour" girl

"The Legend of Sleepy Hollow," by Washington Irving

Why did Washington Irving's famous horseman always do his best at school?

to get "a head" (ahead)

What did Washington Irving's famous horseman do when he panicked?

He lost his head.

Little House Series, by Laura Ingalls Wilder

What popular book tells the story of a pioneer rodent?

Little "Mouse" on the Prairie

What would you get if you crossed Laura Ingalls Wilder with a cow?

Little House on the "Dairy"

The Littles Series, by John Petersen

What do the Littles eat for breakfast?

"Wee-ties" (Wheaties)

See "St. Patrick's Day" in chapter 13, substituting "the Littles" for "leprechauns" when answers involve being short.

The Lord of the Rings Trilogy, by J. R. R. Tolkien

Why do people want to read all of Tolkien's books over and over again?

They're "Hobbit-forming."

What did the Tolkien fan name his telephone answering service?

Lord of the "Rings"

Magic Tree House Series, by Mary Pope Osborne

Where do Jack and Annie get all the candy they can eat?

The Magic "Treat" House

Mrs. Frisby and the Rats of NIMH, by Robert C. O'Brien

What does NIMH call its annual track meet?

the "rat race"

Peter Pan, by James M. Barrie

What Chinese bear doesn't want to grow up?

Peter "Pan-da"

What did Tinker Bell use for cooking?

a Peter "pan"

What did Peter Pan call his fairy when she stopped taking baths?

"Stinker Bell"

Raggedy Ann Series, by Johnny Gruelle

What would you get if you crossed a fictional girl detective with Raggedy Ann?

Nancy "Droop"

What happened to the movie about Raggedy Ann?

It "flopped."

Ramona Series, by Beverly Cleary

What storybook character do ghosts like best?

"Ra-moan-a"

What did Beezus call Ramona when she sat on the stairs?

her "step-sister"

Make this fit other books by substituting the names of other fictional siblings.

What would Beezus and Ramona have been if their aunt had held her wedding in a bakery?

"flour" girls

Ribsy, by Beverly Cleary

What's the skeleton's favorite dog story?

"Rib-sy"

"Rip Van Winkle," by Washington Irving

What storybook character slept in his clothes?

Rip Van "Wrinkled"

What star is named after a famous storybook character?

Rip Van "Twinkle"

Why was Rip Van Winkle scared of going to the library after his twenty-year nap?

His books were way overdue.

The Search for Delicious, by Natalie Babbitt

What day of the week was it when everyone agreed that "water" was the best definition for "delicious"?

"Thirst-day"

Shiloh, by Phyllis Reynolds Naylor

What Newbery Award winner did Phyllis Reynolds Naylor write about a bashful dog?

"Shy-loh"

Tarzan, by Edgar Rice Burroughs

Where does Tarzan keep in shape?

the "jungle gym"

Treasure Island, by Robert Louis Stevenson

How did Jim Hawkins say good-bye to the pirate captain?

"So long, John Silver."

See also "Pirates" in chapter 16.

The Trumpet of the Swan, by E. B. White

What did E. B. White's Louie win a medal for at the swimming meet?

swan dives

Twenty Thousand Leagues under the Sea, by Jules Verne

Why does *Twenty Thousand Leagues under the Sea* give readers a lot to think about?

> It's very "deep."

What did Jules Verne call his novel about a submarine full of frogs?

> *Twenty Thousand "Leaps" under the Sea*

Vampires Don't Wear Polka Dots, by Debbie Dadey and Marcia Thornton Jones

What did the vampire do when she became a teacher?

> She gave "blood tests."

See also "Vampires" in chapter 12.

Winnie-the-Pooh, by A. A. Milne

What does Winnie-the-Pooh have in common with Alexander the Great?

> the same middle name

What did Christopher Robin name his pet skunk?

> Winnie-the-"Pew"

Who likes honey, has a friend named Christopher Robin, and can disappear without a trace?

> Winnie-the-"Poof"

What did Eeyore have when Winnie-the-Pooh gave him a boomerang for his birthday?

> "many happy returns of the day"

What did guests play at Eeyore's birthday party?

> "Pin the Tail on the Host"

Why won't Christopher Robin accept checks from Tigger?

> They might "bounce."

The Wonderful Wizard of Oz, by L. Frank Baum

Why did the critic think *The Wonderful Wizard of Oz* was amazing?

> It blew her away!

What's cold-blooded, has scales and a long tail, and lives in the Emerald City?

> the "lizard" of Oz

What wiggled and jiggled when Dorothy and her friends walked on it?

> the "Jell-O" Brick Road

What card was the Tin Woodman hoping to draw when he played Crazy Eights?

> He wanted a "heart."

What did Dorothy's cowardly lion friend eat on his birthday?

> a "yellow" cake

What happened when Dorothy sent the witch a warm and loving valentine?

> She melted her heart.

Who plays croquet with a broomstick?

> the "Wicket" Witch of the West

MYSTERY SERIES

In General

Fill in the blanks with any fictional detective's name.

How does [name a fictional duck] solve the mysteries he/she reads?

> by "de-duck-tion"

What does _____ put on his/her toothbrush?

> "sleuth-paste"

How did _____ find the lost train?

He/she followed its "tracks."

Why should _____ carry potatoes when he's/she's looking for clues?

They keep their eyes "peeled."

What vegetable helped _____ solve a mystery?

a "clue-cumber"

Why did _____ go to the zoo to study his/her notes on the case?

He/she needed to read between the "lions."

What does _____ do at bedtime?

He/she goes "under covers."

Why did _____ figure the Tupperware saleswoman couldn't have committed the crime?

She had an airtight alibi.

Why did _____ sit on his/her luggage?

He/she was on the "case."

What case did _____ have to sleep on?

the "pillow case"

What did _____ say when he/she found out who stole the museum's mummy?

"That 'wraps' up the case."

Cam Jansen Series, by David A. Adler

Who solves mysteries, has a photographic memory, and lives in the sea?

"Clam" Jansen

Nancy Drew Series, by Carolyn Keene

What did Nancy do when George and Bess asked her to sketch the crime scene?

Nancy "drew."

What fictional girl detective has poor posture?

Nancy "Droop"

Nate the Great Series, by Marjorie Weinman Sharmat

What's round and purple and solves mysteries with his dog, Sludge?

Nate the "Grape"

See also mystery riddles under "Authors" in chapter 7.

NONFICTION

Guinness World Records

Why did the tornado get mentioned in *Guinness*?

It set a "whirl" record.

What book keeps track of how many car crashes take place around the world?

Guinness World "Wreck-ords"

Why did the girl who accidentally dropped her grandma's old phonograph album get into *Guinness*?

She broke a "record."

Humphrey, the Lost Whale: A True Story, by Wendy Tokuda

What would you get if you crossed Humphrey with a bottle of Clorox?

a "bleached" whale

The Magic School Bus Series, by Joanna Cole

What happened when one of Ms. Frizzle's students tied everyone's shoelaces together?

They went on another class "trip."

What's yellow with black stripes, makes honey, and takes Ms. Frizzle's students on amazing trips to beehives and flower gardens?

The Magic School "Buzz"

NURSERY RHYMES

Mother Goose

Who made many mistakes while writing nursery rhymes?

Mother "Goofs"

"Baa, Baa, Black Sheep"

What bleats, has three bags of wool, and is dull and boring?

"Blah, Blah, Black Sheep"

"Georgie Porgie"

What would you get if you crossed a piece of chocolate candy with Georgie Porgie?

a Hershey's Kiss

"Hey, Diddle, Diddle"

See reproducible Mother Goose riddles for dish puppets in appendix C.

"Hickory, Dickory, Dock"

Who takes care of the mouse that ran up the clock when it's sick?

the hickory-dickory "doc"

Where does the mouse that ran up the clock park its boat?

the hickory-dickory dock

How will we know if the mouse runs up the clock again?

"Time will tell."

How did the clock feel when the mouse insulted it?

"ticked off"

Why doesn't Mother Goose leave the clock at the top of the stairs?

It might "run down."

"Humpty Dumpty"

What happened when Humpty Dumpty set off firecrackers on the wall?

He fell down and went boom.

Why did Humpty Dumpty have a great fall?

His favorite team won the World Series.

How did Humpty Dumpty get started on a new hobby?

He "fell into it."

What happened when all the king's horses and all the king's men played an April Fools' Day joke on Humpty Dumpty?

He "fell for it."

Why is Humpty Dumpty getting terrible grades?

He's "falling behind."

Why did the criminals ask Humpty Dumpty to help them rob a bank?

They wanted a "fall guy."

Why did Humpty Dumpty go to the library?

to borrow a "yolk" book

What happened when Humpty Dumpty read a riddle book?

He "cracked up."

Why does Humpty Dumpty need to borrow money from Mother Goose?

He's "broke."

Why does Humpty Dumpty enjoy eating in Chinese restaurants?

He likes egg drop soup.

See also "Eggs" in chapter 16.

"Jack and Jill"

What do Jack and Jill drink to stay healthy?

"well" water

What did Jack and Jill get when they threw jogging shoes into the well?

"running" water

Why did Jack and Jill win a blue ribbon in gymnastics?

They're good at "tumbling."

"Jack Be Nimble"

How can Mother Goose tell when Jack Be Nimble is really happy?

He jumps for joy.

What would you get if you crossed Jack Be Nimble with what another Jack traded for a cow?

jumping beans

What would you get if you crossed Jack Be Nimble with a vine?

a jump rope

What does the nursery rhyme character who leaps over candlesticks do in PE?

jumping Jacks

"Jack Sprat"

Why did Jack Sprat and his wife eat on a seesaw?

to "balance" their diet

What did Jack Sprat and his wife eat after they got a platter having four sides of equal length?

"square meals"

"Little Bo Peep"

How did Little Bo Peep call for her missing sheep?

"Where are 'ewe'?"

Who lives in Mother Goose Land, has a flock of sheep, and cheats at hide-and-seek?

Little Bo "Peeps"

Why did the police suspect Little Bo Peep had taken part in the big sheep robbery?

She'd last been seen with a "crook."

What's harder to find than Little Bo Peep's lost sheep?

a needle in Little Boy Blue's haystack

"Little Boy Blue"

Who blows a horn, sleeps under a haystack, and haunts Mother Goose Land?

Little Boy "Boo!"

What happened when the nursery rhyme character who fell asleep under a haystack had a stuffy nose?

Little Boy "blew."

What nursery rhyme character held his breath too long?

Little Boy Blue

Why does Mother Goose have trouble holding a conversation around Little Boy Blue?

He "horns" in.

When will Mother Goose ask Little Boy Blue to blow his horn?

on New Year's Eve

See also "Little Bo Peep."

"Little Jack Horner"

What did Little Jack Horner eat in geometry class?

his Christmas "pi"

What did Little Jack Horner pull out of his sink?

a plumber

Why couldn't the mouse escape from Little Jack Horner?

He "cornered" it.

"Little Miss Muffet"

Who lost the baseball game for Mother Goose's team?

Little Miss "Muffed-it"

What does Mother Goose order when she eats breakfast at McDonald's?

Egg "McMuffets"

Why did Little Miss Muffet need a map?

She lost her "whey."

Why did Little Miss Muffet think the spider was a nuisance?

It got in her "whey."

What did Little Miss Muffet tell the spider when it asked for a bite of her food?

"No 'whey'!"

Why did Wee Willie Winkie always carry around a bowl of Miss Muffet's food?

Where there's a "Will," there's a "whey."

When did the spider sit down beside Miss Muffet?

when it "spied-'er"

"Mary Had a Little Lamb"

What did the little lamb ride on when it followed the girl to an amusement park?

the "Mary-go-round"

Why do the little lamb and the girl it follows enjoy December every year?

They always have a "Mary" Christmas.

"Mary, Mary, Quite Contrary"

What did contrary Mary have when she buried money in her garden?

"rich" soil

"Old King Cole"

What merry old soul is never warm?

Old King "Cold"

What merry old soul lives underground?

Old King "Coal"

"Old Mother Hubbard"

What seven letters did Old Mother Hubbard say when she saw that her cupboard was bare?

"O I C U R M T."

What did the dog get from Old Mother Hubbard's freezer?

an ice-cream "bone"

"Old Woman Who Lived in a Shoe"

Why will the old woman and her children have to move out of the shoe?

It's being "soled" (sold).

What kind of music does the old woman who lives in the shoe enjoy?

"sole" music

"Peter, Peter, Pumpkin Eater"

What did Peter, Peter's wife use to mend the crack in her wall?

a pumpkin "patch"

"The Queen of Hearts"

What would the Queen of Hearts have if she put firecrackers in her pastries?

Pop!-Tarts

"Rub-a-Dub-Dub"

What happened to the three men in the tub when it overturned?

They got wet.

How did the baker get rich?

He made lots of "dough."

Why do the butcher, the baker, and the candlestick maker want to lose weight?

They're "tubby."

"Three Blind Mice"

Where can the three blind mice get new tails?

a "re-tail" store

Why can't the three blind mice be authors?

They have no "tales."

"Tom, Tom, the Piper's Son"

How did the police know that the piper's son stole the pig?

The pig "squealed."

"Wee Willie Winkie"

What nursery rhyme character wears a nightgown, runs around town, and keeps blinking one eye?

Wee Willie "Winker"

See also "Little Miss Muffet."

 **The Loony Library**

*Riddles for Loony Library
Bulletin Boards and Games*

These silly imaginary books by pretend authors work with bulletin boards in chapter 1 as well as card games, "Find Your Partner," and "The Loony Library Book Hunt" in chapter 3. If necessary, change call numbers to fit your classification system. (See the cards in appendix C for more titles and authors.)

Who wrote *Animals of the Desert*? (591.909 A)

Jack R. Abbott

Who wrote *The Life and Works of Beatrix Potter*? (B POT)

Peter R. Abbott

Who wrote *Playing Keyboard Instruments*? (786.19 A)

P. Anno

Who wrote *All about the Sun*? (523.7 A)

Ray D. Ant

Who wrote *All about Michigan*? (977.4 A)

Ann Arbor

Who wrote *The Man behind the Lord of the Rings*? (B TOL)

Bill Bo Baggins

Who wrote *Delicious Cakes for You to Make*? (641.865 B)

Bea A. Baker

Who wrote *Historic Farm Buildings*? (631.22 B)

Red Barnes

Who wrote *Henry Ford and the Model T*? (B FOR)

Otto Moe Beal

Who wrote *Where the Tide Comes In*? (574.92 B)

Sandy Beech

Who wrote *Danger in the Ocean*? (551.3 B)

I. C. E. Berg

Who wrote *Making Christmas Wreaths*? (745.594 B)

Holly Berry

Who wrote *Cycling across the United States?* (F BIK)

    Rhoda Bike

Who wrote *The Curse of the Werewolf?* (F BOD)

    Harry Boddy

Who wrote *Crossing the River?* (624.2 B)

    I. Ron Bridges

Who wrote *Insects in Your Yard?* (595.7 B)

    June Bugg

Who wrote *My Life as a Lumberjack?* (B BUR)

    Tim Burr

Who wrote *Feathered Friends in Your Backyard?* (598.072 B)

    Jay Byrd

Who wrote *What My Dog Likes to Do?* (E CAR)

    Chase A. Carr

Who wrote *What Do Teachers Do?* (372.11 C)

    Ed U. Cate

Who wrote *The Mystery in the Sandwich Shop?* (F CAT)

    Del I. Catessen

Who wrote *Learn How to Draw?* (743 C)

    Art Class

Who wrote *My PE Teacher Is an Alien?* (F CLA)

    Jim Class

Who wrote *When I Got Glasses?* (617.7 C)

    I. Seymour Clearly

Who wrote *Storms in the Midwest?* (551.55 C)

    Cy Clone

Who wrote *Snakes of South America?* (597.96 C)

    Anna Conda

Who wrote *Conversations with Award-Winning Illustrators?* (741.642 C)

    Cal D. Cott

Who wrote *When I Get Mad?* (E CRO)

    I. M. Cross

Who wrote *The Story of Clara Barton?* (B BAR)

    Red Cross

Who wrote *Exploring the Everglades?* (975.9 D)

    Flora Da

Who wrote *What Beavers Do?* (599.37 D)

    Bill D. Dam

Who wrote *Just a Light Rain?* (551.57 D)

    Misty Day

Who wrote *How to Plant a Tree?* (635.977 D)

    R. Burr Day

Who wrote *Let's Go Fly a Kite?* (E DAY)

    Wynn D. Day

Who wrote *My Best Friend?* (F DEE)

    Bud Dee

Who wrote *Singing in Harmony?* (783 D)

    Mel O. Dee

Who wrote *I'll Try Anything?* (B DEW)

    Will Dew

Who wrote *On the Job with a Construction Worker*? (690 D)

    Bill Ding

Who wrote *My Life as an Illustrator*? (741.642 D)

    I. Drew

Who wrote *The Visitor from Outer Space*? (F ENN)

    A. Lee Enn

Who wrote *The Scariest Stories You've Ever Read*? (F FID)

    Tara Fide

Who wrote *Mr. Bell and His Invention*? (B BEL)

    T. Ella Fone

Who wrote *Norman Bridwell and His Big Red Dog*? (B BRI)

    Cliff Ford

Who wrote *The Golden State*? (979.4 F)

    Cal I. Fornia

Who wrote *The Biggest Animal on Land*? (599.67 F)

    Ella Funt

Who wrote *Creatures of the Swamp*? (597.98 G)

    Allie Gator

Who wrote *My Favorite Color*? (E GRE)

    Kelly Green

Who wrote *Living in a Pigsty*? (636.4 H)

    Ima Hogg

Who wrote *Camping in an RV*? (F HOM)

    Moe Bill Home

Who wrote *At Home with the Third Little Pig*? (E HOW)

    B. Rick Howes

Who wrote *Felines of the World*? (636.8 K)

    Kitty Katz

Who wrote *Riding Horses to Win*? (798.4 K)

    Jock Key

Who wrote *You Can Be a Comedian*? (792.7028 K)

    Joe King

Who wrote *Things to Do with Rope*? (623.88 K)

    Ty Knotts

Who wrote *The Smallest State in the Union*? (974.5 L)

    Rhoda I. Land

Who wrote *The Colors of Fall*? (508.2 L)

    Autumn Leaf

Who wrote *Vegetables Are Good for You*? (613.2 L)

    Brock O. Lee

Who wrote *Without a Cent*? (F LES)

    Penny Less

Who wrote *Identifying Wildflowers*? (635.9 L)

    Vi O. Letts

Who wrote *Yummy Desserts for You to Make*? (641.8 L)

    Dee Licious

Who wrote *Songs to Sing at Christmas*? (782.28 L)

    Carol Ling

Who wrote *King Arthur's Knights*? (398.2 L)
Lance A. Lott

Who wrote *Communicating through Computers*? (384.34 M)
E. Mail

Who wrote *All about Amphibians*? (597.8 M)
Sally Mander

Who wrote *The Race Is about to Begin*? (E MAR)
Anya Marks

Who wrote *When Santa Claus Comes*? (E MAS)
Chris T. Mas

Who wrote *How They Make Cartoons*? (791.43 M)
Anna Mate

Who wrote *What You Need for Wrestling*? (796.8 M)
Jim Matt

Who wrote *My Life Underground*? (B MIN)
Cole Miner

Who wrote *How to Get Smart*? (371.3 M)
Reed Moore

Who wrote *Animals of Madagascar*? (599.83 M)
Lee Murr

Who wrote *Tracking Twisters*? (551.55 N)
Torey Nado

Who wrote *How Bees Help Flowers*? (582 N)
Polly Nation

Who wrote *Sounds in a Haunted House*? (F NIN)
Moe Ning

Who wrote *The Land of Lincoln*? (977.3 N)
Ella Noy

Who wrote *Riding Bulls and Roping Calves*? (791.8 O)
Roe D. Oh

Who wrote *What We Get from the Sun*? (523.7 O)
Ray O'Sunshine

Who wrote *Doing It Over*? (F PET)
Ria Pete

Who wrote *I Was an Illustrator*? (B PIC)
Drew Pictures

Who wrote *Using Good Manners*? (395 P)
Mae I. Please

Who wrote *Where Penguins Live*? (919.8 P)
S. Pole

Who wrote *The Amazing Adventures of Spider-Man*? (F POW)
Sue Purr Powers

Who wrote *Trees in the Swamp*? (574.5 P)
Cy Press

Who wrote *Yellowstone National Park*? (917.87 R)
Forrest Ranger

Who wrote *Making Your Own Bracelets*? (745.594 R)
Jewel Ree

Who wrote *How to Jump Double Dutch?* (796.2 R)

Skip N. Rope

Who wrote *Prehistoric Reptiles?* (567.9 S)

Dinah Saur

Who wrote *Lots of Games for Kids to Play?* (790 S)

Simon Says

Who wrote *Traveling through China?* (915.1 S)

Rick Shaw

Who wrote *Fancy Basketball Plays?* (796.323 S)

T. Rick Shott

Who wrote *All about Blizzards?* (551.55 S)

Lotta Snow

Who wrote *The Wizard of Menlo Park?* (B EDI)

Ed I. Son

Who wrote *The Mystery in the Stables?* (F STA)

Horace Stahl

Who wrote *The Kid Who Went to Hollywood?* (E STA)

Bea A. Starr

Who wrote *Confessions of a Shoplifter?* (B STE)

I. Steel

Who wrote *A Cowboy's Job?* (978 S)

Brandon Steers

Who wrote *The Most Frightening Book You've Ever Read?* (F STO)

S. Carrie Story

Who wrote *Behind the Scenes at the Ballet?* (792.8 S)

Dan Surr

Who wrote *Cinderella and Other Princess Stories?* (398.2 T)

Faye Ria Tales

Who wrote *The Biggest Ship Ever?* (910.9 T)

Ty Tannic

Who wrote *How to Solve Crimes?* (652.8 T)

Dee Tective

Who wrote *Preparing for Quizzes?* (371.26 T)

Tess Ting

Who wrote *Growing What You Eat?* (635 T)

Tom A. To

Who wrote *Ballerina for a Day?* (792.8 T)

Anya Toes

Who wrote *How a Lightbulb Works?* (621.3 T)

E. Lex Tricity

Who wrote *The Bluegrass State?* (976.9 T)

Ken Tucky

Who wrote *The Most Suspenseful Story You've Ever Read?* (F TUR)

Paige Turner

Who wrote *A Holiday in February?* (394.2618 T)

Val N. Tyne

Who wrote *Emily and the Blackbird?* (E VEN)

Ray Venn

Who wrote *When Brother Fought Brother*?
(973.7 W)

    Cybil War

Who wrote *Traveling the Oregon Trail*? (978 W)

    Wes T. Ward

Who wrote *Let's Go to an Amusement Park*?
(791.068 W)

    Ferris Wheel

10 Merry Menagerie

Riddles about Animals and Zoos

GENERIC ANIMAL RIDDLES

Fill in the blanks with the animals' names.

Any Animal

What follows a _____ wherever it goes?

   its tail

What does a _____ have that no other animal has?

   baby _____s

What is a baby _____ after it's five days old?

   six days old

What side of a _____ has the most fur [feathers, scales]?

   the outside

When do _____s have eight legs?

   when there are two of them

Any Animal That Hops

What do _____s eat for breakfast?

   "Hop-Tarts"

What would you call a _____ that got stuck in the mud?

   "un-hoppy"

What do _____s like best about fairy tales?

   the "hoppy" endings

What would you get if you crossed a _____ with a snake?

   a jump rope

Why do _____s make poor decisions?

   They "jump" to conclusions.

Why will the basketball referee blow the whistle on the tired _____?

   It's out of "bounds."

Any Animal with Spots

Why did the _____ have red spots?

  It had chicken pox.

Why don't _____s like to play hide-and-seek?

  They're always "spotted."

Why will the _____ go to the eye doctor?

  It's seeing spots.

Why will the _____ take its coat to the clean-ers?

  It's covered with spots.

Create new riddles with "spot" in the answer.

Any Amphibian

What would you call a _____ that tells lies?

  an "am-fib-ian"

What kind of amphibian has three legs?

  a "toad-stool"

What game do tired amphibians play?

  "sleep" frog

What do amphibians read every day?

  the "newts-paper"

Any Fish or Reptile

Why did the _____ do well in music class?

  It already knew its "scales."

Why is it easy to weigh a _____?

  They have their own "scales."

Any Mammal

Why do _____s have fur coats?

  Plastic raincoats don't come in their size.

What did the _____ plant on Arbor Day?

  a "fur" (fir) tree

Any Reptile

What do _____s put on their kitchen floors?

  "rep-tiles"

BIRDS

Why do [name a kind of bird] forget every-thing?

  They're "bird-brains."

What would you get if you crossed a Scottish sea creature with a bird's home?

  the Loch "Nest" Monster

How do we know that birds take risks?

  They'll "go out on a limb."

Why do bad-tempered birds always get plenty to eat?

  The "surly" bird catches the worm.

Why don't most readers understand the book about how birds fly?

  It's over their heads.

What do you call a [name a kind of bird] when it's ten below zero?

  a "brrrr-d"

What did the early bird catch at the library?

  a "book-worm"

CREEPY CRAWLIES

In General

What do the insects call their pet rabbit?

  "bugs' bunny"

Why did the spies hire an exterminator?

>   Their room was "bugged."

Where can you buy insects?

>   "flea" markets

What has six legs and wings, flies, and can't stand Christmas?

>   a "hum-bug"

What kinds of insects have two legs, no wings, and make a mess?

>   "litter-bugs"

Ants

What insects are very old and valuable?

>   "ant-iques"

What's the world's biggest insect?

>   a "gi-ant"

What insect has a long, gray trunk?

>   an "eleph-ant"

Create new riddles with "ant" in the answer. Get ideas from Cathi Hepworth's ANTics! *and Bernard Most's* There's an Ant in Anthony.

Where do ants play football?

>   in a "sugar bowl"

Bees

When might your report card sting you?

>   when it's all "bees"

What do bees like to chew?

>   "bumble-gum"

What's yellow with black stripes, makes honey, and drops the football all the time?

>   a "fumble-bee"

What's yellow with black stripes, makes honey, and trips over flowers?

>   a "stumble-bee"

Create new riddles using words that rhyme with "bumble."

Why did the bumblebee go to the doctor [or dermatologist]?

>   It had "hives."

Why do beekeepers have sticky heads?

>   They use "honey-combs."

What insects are fun to play with?

>   "Fris-bees"

Where do honeybees sleep at night?

>   flower "beds"

What would you call two bees, a wasp, and a hornet playing musical instruments?

>   a "sting" quartet

Butterflies and Caterpillars

What's beautiful, has six legs, and tastes good on toast?

>   "butter-flies"

Why did eating caterpillars make the bird nervous?

>   It got butterflies in its stomach.

Fireflies

Why do fireflies get As in school?

>   They're very "bright."

How do fireflies learn arithmetic?

>   with "flash" cards

What helps fireflies see in the dark?

"flash-lights"

What must little fireflies do before they're allowed to go out at night?

"glow" up

What did the hungry lizard call the firefly?

a "light" snack

What would you call a lightning bug that lost its job?

a "fired-fly"

See also chapter 15.

Ladybugs

What insects have good manners?

"lady-bugs"

What kind of insects do Boy Scouts help across the street?

"old lady-bugs"

See also "Any Animal with Spots."

Spiders

What do frogs and toads drink in the fall?

apple "spider"

What scatterbrained creature climbed up the waterspout?

the itsy, "ditzy" spider

Why did the spider go to the doctor?

It caught a "bug."

What was the spider doing in the outfield?

catching "flies"

What do spiders eat with hamburgers?

french "flies"

What should you do if you find a tarantula in your sneakers?

Wear your flip-flops.

What will you get if a spider makes its home on your shoes?

"webbed" feet

What will you get if a spider makes its home in your library book?

"web pages"

What do spiders eat at summer cookouts?

corn on the "cob-web"

What computer class did the spider teach at the library?

Building Your Own "Web Page"

Why do spiders spin webs?

They can't crochet.

How did the spider do on its spinning test?

It got a "bee."

What goes "ouch, ouch, ouch, ouch, ouch, ouch, ouch, ouch"?

a spider whose shoes are too tight

What do you say to a spider before it acts in a play?

"Break a leg, leg, leg, leg, leg, leg, leg, leg."

Worms

What did the early bird catch at the library?

a "book-worm"

What's worse than finding a worm in your apple?

> finding half a worm

Why do we measure worms in inches?

> They have no feet.

What animal hates the metric system?

> an inchworm

What worm [or annelid] can make you black-and-blue?

> a "pinch-worm"

What's wiggly, has no legs, and tried to steal Christmas?

> a "Grinch-worm"

Create new riddles using words that rhyme with "inch."

What kind of worms served in King Arthur's court?

> "knight" crawlers

What do night crawlers do when they get into trouble?

> "worm" their way out

Why do smart earthworms sleep in?

> to avoid early birds

Where do earthworms get mail?

> the "compost" office

What kind of gum do earthworms chew?

> "Wiggly's" Spearmint

See also bookworm riddles under "Books"— "Reference Books"—"Dictionary" and "Libraries" in chapter 7.

DINOSAURS AND PTERODACTYLS

Where did dinosaurs sleep?

> on "bed-rock"

What kind of fossils lie in bedrock?

> "lazy bones"

Why didn't the dinosaur cross the road?

> There weren't any roads.

What prehistoric reptiles were black-and-blue?

> "dino-sores"

What prehistoric reptiles made noise while they slept?

> "dino-snores"

Why did the apatosaurus eat the factory?

> It was a "plant" eater.

What prehistoric animals flew around scaring everybody?

> "terror-dactyls"

What did stegosauruses do during volleyball games?

> "spiked" the ball

What dinosaur had its own dishes?

> Stegosaurus had "plates."

What slogan did the three-horned dinosaur use to advertise the shirts she made?

> "Try Sarah's Tops."

What dinosaurs never stopped spinning around?

> "tricera-tops"

Why did prehistoric animals have trouble holding conversations around a triceratops?

It "horned" in.

How did a triceratops make noise on New Year's Eve?

It blew its "horns."

What dinosaur played golf?

"Tee-rex"

What dinosaur made a mess out of everything?

Tyrannosaurus "wrecks"

DRAGONS

What did the knight get when the dragon sneezed?

out of the way

What did the fire-breathing dragon call the brave knight?

"toast"

What did the dragon call the knight in shining armor?

canned food

When did the dragon get full?

around "mid-knight"

What time is it when a dragon captures a princess?

"knight-time"

PETS

Any Pet in a Cage

What did the baseball slugger buy his pet _____?

a "batting cage"

Any Small Rodent

What happened when the kids put their _____ in their remote-controlled plane?

They watched the fur fly.

Birds

ANY PET BIRD

How did the sick _____ get to the vet?

It "flu."

What did the veterinarian give the sick _____?

"tweetment"

What did the silly kids do when they wanted a pet _____?

They planted birdseed.

What kind of fish lives in birdcages?

a "perch"

CANARIES

Why is the canary afraid of the vet?

It's "yellow."

What do canaries eat for breakfast?

Cream of "Tweet"

Why did the kids save money when they bought a canary?

It was going "cheep."

What did the canary call its Rollerblades?

"cheep skates"

PARROTS

What does Polly want on the Fourth of July?

a "fire-cracker"

What did the hungry parrot say?

"Long time, no 'seed.'"

When are your teeth like a talkative parrot?

when they "chatter"

What would you get if you crossed a parrot with a poisonous reptile?

a "prattle-snake"

What would you get if you crossed a parrot with the post office?

voice mail

What would you get if you crossed a parrot with a yak?

a yakkety-yak

Cats

Why is it hard to talk when your kitten bites the middle of your sneaker?

The cat's got your "tongue."

Why did the cat win the race?

It was good in the long "stretch."

Why do cats have whiskers?

Without hands, it's hard to shave.

Which kitten cheated on the test?

the "copy-cat"

Where do cats go when they want to have fun?

"a-mew-sement" parks

What would you call a flying saucer filled with cats from outer space?

a "Mew-FO"

Create new riddles with "mew" in the answer.

What did the cat say when someone stepped on its tail?

"Me-OW!"

What kind of cat helps the school nurse?

the first-aid "kit"

How can you tell if a cat burglar visited your house?

Your cat is missing.

What's a contented cat's favorite color?

"purr-ple"

What do cats wear when they want to smell nice?

"purr-fume"

Create new riddles with "purr" in the answer.

What do black cats eat for breakfast?

"Un-Lucky" Charms

What did the cats say when they saw the skateboarding mice?

"Look! Meals on Wheels!"

What did the polite cat say when it met a mouse?

"It's a pleasure to 'eat' you."

What would you call a cat that eats lemons?

a "sour-puss"

What kind of cat has eight legs?

an "octo-puss"

What kind of cats actually like water?

"cat-fish"

What would you call your couch if your cat shed on it?

"furr-niture"

What did the cat lose when the little girl stood up?

her lap

How do space cats drink milk?

from flying "saucers"

What's special about the new postage stamp with a picture of a cat on it?

It licks itself.

See also "Summer" in chapter 13 and the pet bookmark in appendix C.

Dogs

What should you tell your young dog if it barks too much?

"Hush, puppy."

How can you sneak your puppy into a restaurant?

Hide it in a "doggie" bag.

Why did the dog scratch after shopping with its owners?

They'd gone to "flea" markets.

Why couldn't the dog turn in its homework for obedience school?

Its master ate it.

What kind of dog does a vampire have?

a bloodhound

What dogs get into the most fights?

"boxers"

What kind of pet picks on puppies?

a "bully-dog"

What breed of dog can tell time?

"clocker" spaniels

What does Lassie put in her cakes?

"collie-flour"

How can you tell when wiener dogs enjoy their food?

They eat with "relish."

What dogs keep fire stations clean?

"dal-maid-tians"

Why doesn't the police dog look like a police dog?

It's undercover.

What happened when the watchdog ate garlic and onions?

Its bark was much worse than its bite.

Why did the watchdog go to the vet?

It had "ticks."

How is a puppy on a summer day like something you roast over a bonfire?

It's a "hot dog."

How can you make your dog laugh?

Give it a "funny bone."

What do you call a puppy that chews shoes?

"gnaw-ty"

What should you do if your dog chases everyone on a bike?

Take away its bike.

What do lazy dogs chase?

parked cars

Why is the dog named Matches lonely?

No one's allowed to play with it.

What did the dog say when it sat on sandpaper?

"'Ruff. Ruff.'"

See also "Dogsled Racing" in chapter 14 and the pet and jester bookmarks in appendix C.

Ferrets

Who collects the baby teeth that little weasels lose?

the Tooth "Ferret"

What amusement park ride do pet weasels enjoy?

the "ferrets'" wheel

Fish

What bedtime story should you read to your pet fish?

The Adventures of Huckleberry "Fin"

What kind of pet does Ronald McDonald have?

a "clown-fish"

How did King Midas get his pet goldfish?

He touched a shark.

What did one fish in the tank say to the other fish in the tank?

"Got any idea how to drive this thing?"

Where do goldfish play football?

in the "super bowl"

Guinea Pigs

What pet rodents are greedy?

"gimme" pigs

Hamsters

What would you get if you crossed a frog with Lynne Reid Banks's Houdini (or Betty G. Birney's Humphrey)?

"green legs and ham-ster"

What did the history students call their pet rodent?

"Abra-hamster" Lincoln

Horses

Why is the colt eating cough drops?

It's a little "horse" (hoarse).

Where do horses go to college?

"Hay U"

What do farmers say when they feed their horses?

"'Hay,' you."

What makes the horse sneeze after every meal?

"hay fever"

Why was the king's horse hungry whenever Rumpelstiltskin was around?

>He spun its supper into gold.

What would you get if you crossed [name a fictional horse] with a chameleon?

>a horse of a different color

Why didn't the little horse get permission to play at a friend's house?

>Its mother could only say "neigh" (nay).

What do you call horses whose stalls are next door to each other?

>"neighhhhhhhh-bors"

How can you keep a nervous horse from bolting out of the barn?

>"Stall" it.

Why can the sick horse go home from the animal hospital?

>It's in "stable" condition.

What does the farmer call the horse that keeps begging for food?

>an old "nag"

Why couldn't the horse draw the wagon?

>It didn't have a pencil.

What fruit should you eat when you're riding a horse?

>"canter-lope"

See also chapter 15.

Mice

Why are pet mice noisy after you give them a bath?

>They're "squeaky clean."

What games can you play with your pet mice?

>hide-and-"squeak" and "squeak-a-boo"

How can you keep in touch with your pet mouse when you're away from home?

>Send "squeak-mail."

Why should you give your pet mouse string cheese for dessert?

>to floss its teeth

Rabbits

What pets snatch food out of your hands when you feed them?

>"grabbits"

What's the best way to raise rabbits?

>Pick them up.

Why is breeding rabbits nerve-wracking?

>It's a "hare-raising" experience.

Why does taking care of rabbits make you tired?

>They keep you "hopping."

What do the insects call their pet rabbit?

>"bugs' bunny"

What kinds of rabbits live under your bed?

>"dust bunnies"

What should you read your pet rabbit at bedtime?

>"cotton-tales"

Turtles

How can you keep in touch with your pet turtle when you're away from home?

>Use "shell" phones.

See the activity sheet "Can You Fill In the Blanks?" and the pet bookmark in appendix C for more pet riddles.

WILD ANIMALS

Any Animal with Stripes

What happened when the _____ was court-martialed?

It lost its stripes.

Any Ocean Animal

Why did the _____ cross the ocean?

to get to the other "tide"

How can you contact a _____ by computer?
Send "sea-mail."

Where do _____s sleep at night?

in water beds

What do _____s eat for dessert?

"sponge" cake

Alligators and Crocodiles

How did the alligator feel when it got too much homework?

"swamped"

Who goes bowling in the swamp?

"alley-gators"

Who brought the alligator a cool drink on a hot day?

its "Gator-aide"

What did the alligator/crocodile do when it felt overwhelmed?

It "snapped."

What will you always get if you ask an alligator/crocodile a question?

a "snappy" answer

Antelopes

What do antelopes read every day?

the "gnus-paper"

What do antelopes get for the first day of school?

"gnu" clothes

What kind of cookies do antelopes like?

Fig "Gnu-tons"

Create new riddles with "gnu" in the answer.

What has antlers, lives in Africa, and delivers presents on Christmas Eve?

"Santa-lope"

Ants

See "Creepy Crawlies."

Bats

What holiday do flying mammals celebrate on March 17th?

St. "Bat-rick's" Day

Who was a famous queen, lived in ancient Egypt, and hung upside down in a cave all day?

"Cleo-bat-ra"

What do you call a flying mammal that takes gymnastics lessons?

an "acro-bat"

What did the bat say to the witch's hat?

"You go on 'a head.' I'll 'hang around' here."

What do bats like to do with their friends?

"hang out"

Bears

Why didn't the bear eat the camper wearing a Hawaiian shirt, plaid pants, and loud socks?

He had "bad taste."

What do young bears like to eat for dessert?

"cub-cakes"

Why do bears sleep all winter?

They can't afford alarm clocks.

What would you call it if a bear slept in a tree-top all winter?

"high-bernation"

What would you call a panda without any teeth?

a "gummy" bear

What Chinese bear never wants to grow up?

Peter "Pan-da"

Why did the police arrest the polar bear?

It robbed the snow "bank."

What do polar bears put on their beds?

"sheets" of ice

What do polar bears eat for breakfast?

"Ice" Krispies

What do polar bears eat at McDonald's?

"iceberg-ers"

What do polar bears eat in Mexican restaurants?

"brrr-itos"

See also snow riddles in chapter 16 and reproducible riddles for snowmen puppets in appendix C. Substitute "polar bears" for "snowmen" where appropriate.

Beavers

What would you get if you crossed a beaver with a telephone?

a busy signal

What did the tree get when the beaver chewed it?

a "gnawing" feeling

What did Aladdin's lamp give the beaver?

"tree" wishes

What did the beaver order in the fancy restaurant?

a "tree-course" meal

Bees

See "Creepy Crawlies."

Camels

What would you call a camel's clone?

its "spitting" image

What helps a dromedary hide in the desert?

"camel-flage"

Cheetahs

Why do cheetahs eat at McDonald's?

They like fast food.

What would you get if you crossed a cheetah with a beach?

"quick-sand"

Chimpanzees

What kind of cookies do apes like best?

chocolate "chimp"

What would you get if you crossed an ape with a flower?

a "chimp-pansy"

Crocodiles

See "Alligators and Crocodiles."

Deer

Why did the female deer need a loan from the bank?

She didn't have a "buck."

Why did the male deer go to the orthodontist?

It had "buck" teeth.

What would you get if you crossed a storm cloud with Rudolph?

a "rain-deer"

Dolphins

How do dolphins like their bathwater?

"fluke-warm"

What ocean animals play football?

the Miami Dolphins

Elephants

What's sicker than an elephant with a stuffy nose?

a giraffe with strep throat

Why do elephants have trunks?

They don't have glove compartments.

What would you get if you crossed goldfish with elephants?

swimming trunks

What happened when the elephant jumped in the pool?

It made a big splash.

What would you get if you crossed an elephant with a dictionary?

"big words"

What would you get if you crossed an elephant with a skunk?

a "big stink"

Create new riddles with "big" in the answer.

What's big and gray and really stinks?

a "smell-ephant"

What's big and gray and visits people in hospitals?

the "get well–ephant"

Who's big and gray and wears glass slippers?

"Cinderella-phant"

Create new riddles using words that rhyme with "el."

Why do elephants need loud alarm clocks?

They're "heavy" sleepers.

See also "Any Giant Story" in chapter 8.

Fish

Why do fish swim in salt water?

Pepper makes them sneeze.

What kind of school has no teachers, no students, and no classrooms?

a "school" of fish

How did the fish get to be so smart?

It's always in "school."

Why is the fish swimming at the bottom of the sea?

It dropped out of "school."

What would you get if you crossed goldfish with elephants?

swimming "trunks"

Where do fish keep all their money?

river "banks"

Why did the police arrest the fish?

It robbed the river "bank."

What has a bright red nose, wears big, floppy shoes, and lives in the sea?

a "clown-fish"

Who grants wishes for fishes?

fairy "cod-mothers"

What kind of fish lives in birdcages?

a "perch"

What fish made it big out in Hollywood?

the "star-fish"

What's the difference between a piano and a fish?

You can't "tuna" fish.

Have you ever seen fish cry?

No, but I've seen whales "blubber."

See also "Any Fish or Reptile" and "Pets"— "Fish."

Foxes

What did the fox do when it moved next door to the rabbit?

had its neighbor for supper

Frogs and Toads

What do frogs and toads drink in the fall?

apple "spider"

What do frogs eat with hamburgers?

french "flies"

What was the frog doing in the outfield?

catching "flies"

What's mean and green and picks on little tadpoles?

a "bully-frog"

Who delivers colored eggs and candy to tadpoles each spring?

the Easter "Ribbit"

Why can't frogs and toads be authors?

They have no "tales."

What magazine do toads like to read?

"Warts" Illustrated

What game did the toads play with rope in PE?

"tug-of-warts"

What science fiction movie is about toads in outer space?

Star "Warts"

See also "Any Animal That Hops," as well as "The Frog Prince" in chapter 8.

Giraffes

Why don't giraffes need to eat a lot?

They make a little go a long way.

Why did it take a long time for the giraffe to apologize?

It had to swallow its pride first.

Why do giraffes have long necks?

Their feet really stink.

Why has the giraffe been in the bathtub for ten hours?

It's washing its neck.

How can you tell that giraffes are brave?

They stick their necks out.

What's sicker than an elephant with a stuffy nose?

a giraffe with strep throat

Why do giraffes sing soprano in the chorus?

They can reach the high notes.

What do giraffes like to read?

"tall tales"

Gorillas

When do gorillas fall out of the sky?

during "Ape-ril" showers

Groundhogs

See "Groundhog Day" in chapter 13.

Hippos

What's big, lives in Africa, and is very cool?

the "hip-popotamus"

What's big, lives in Africa, and never stops eating?

a "hippo-bottomless"

What's big, lives in Africa, and has chicken pox?

a "hippo-spot-amus"

Hyenas

What would you get if you crossed a laughing hyena with a cat?

a giggle puss

See also "Zoos."

Kangaroos

Why do mother kangaroos hate when it rains?

Their kids have to play inside.

What do you call little kangaroos that never play outside?

"pouch" potatoes

Why did the kangaroo put Band-Aids on its pouch?

It babysat a porcupine.

See also "Any Animal That Hops" and "Zoos."

Koalas

Why do mother koalas have pouches?

Pushing strollers in trees is impossible.

Leopards

See "Any Animal with Spots."

Lions

Why did the lion cross the savannah?

to get to the other "pride"

Why shouldn't you make fun of a lion family?

You'll hurt their "pride."

What steps should you take if you see an escaped lion?

very long ones

Why can't you believe everything the king of the jungle tells you?

He's always "lyin'."

How does the king of the jungle catch prey?

by "lyin'" in wait

Where do lions live?

on "Mane" Street

What does the ringmaster call the circus's lion-taming act?

"our 'mane' attraction"

Why do lions eat raw meat?

They can't read cookbooks.

What happened when the lion read a riddle book?

It "roared" with laughter.

Mice

Why are mice never safe during thunderstorms?

It "rains cats and dogs."

How did the mouse do on the test?

It "squeaked" by.

When does a mouse weigh as much as an elephant?

when the scale is broken

What kind of mouse doesn't like cheese?

a computer "mouse"

What do mice eat on their birthdays?

"cheese-cake"

Why did the mouse follow the photographer?

It heard her say, "Cheese!"

What animal is gray and has a trunk?

a mouse on summer vacation

See also "Cats" and "Mice" under "Pets."

Monkeys

Where do monkeys keep in shape?

the "jungle gym"

Why are the bananas afraid of the monkey?

They're "yellow."

See also "Zoos," as well as "Curious George Series" in chapter 8.

Octopuses

What would you get if you crossed an eight-armed sea creature with a cat?

an "octo-puss"

What would you get if you crossed an electric eel with an eight-armed sea creature?

a "shocked-opus"

What has eight arms, lives in the ocean, and tells time?

a "clock-topus"

What can bang on your door with eight arms?

a "knock-topus"

Create new riddles using words that rhyme with "ock."

Why does an octopus have suckers?

    It's allergic to chocolate.

What would you get if you crossed a jacket with an octopus?

    a "coat of arms"

Why isn't the octopus afraid to go into battle?

    It's "well-armed."

Otters

Who has a magic wand, plays Quidditch, and lives in the sea?

    Harry "Otter"

Porcupines

What animals are always broke?

    "poor-cupines"

What would you get if a porcupine sat on your sofa?

    a pincushion

What do porcupines put on their hamburgers?

    dill "prickles"

Why don't porcupines have birthday parties?

    They'd pop the balloons.

Why did the kangaroo put Band-Aids on its pouch?

    It babysat a porcupine.

Rabbits

What bunnies fix flat tires?

    "jack-rabbits"

How are rabbits like cornstalks?

    They have big "ears."

What would you get if you poured boiling water down a rabbit hole?

    "hot, cross bunnies"

What keeps rabbits cool in summer?

    "hare-conditioning"

What did the rabbit have when it got up on the wrong side of the bed?

    a bad "hare" day

Why did the bald man put a rabbit on his head?

    to have a full head of "hare"

What would you call a row of rabbits hopping backward?

    a receding "hare-line"

Who goes to Hogwarts, plays Quidditch, and has very long ears?

    "Hare-y" Potter

Create new riddles using "hare" for "hair."

How did the rabbit feel when somebody stole its carrots?

    "hopping mad"

How do you know carrots are good for your eyes?

    Rabbits never wear glasses.

What did the rabbit call the carrot that insulted it?

    a "fresh" vegetable

What do rabbits like to read?

    "cotton-tales"

*See also "Any Animal That Hops" and "Pets"—
"Rabbits," as well as chapter 15.*

Rats

Why is the rat sad?

It's down in the dumps.

What rodents can help you get ready to move?

"pack" rats

What do rodents call their marathon?

the "rat race"

Rhinoceroses

What lives in Africa, has a horn, and fusses all
the time?

a "whine-oceros"

*See also "Dinosaurs and Pterodactyls," substituting
"rhino" for "triceratops" where appropriate.*

Seals

Why is making pancakes easy for seals?

They have their own "flippers."

What's round, lives in the Oval Office of the
White House, and eats fish?

the presidential "seal"

What lives in the ocean, eats fish, and claps its
flippers when something is good?

the "seal" of approval

See also "Circuses" in chapter 16.

Sharks

How did King Midas get his pet goldfish?

He touched a shark.

Why was the shark smart?

It ate "schools" of fish.

What's worse than seeing a shark's fin heading
toward you when you're swimming?

seeing its tonsils

What do you call a man who stuck his right
arm in a shark's mouth?

"Lefty"

Why won't sharks eat clowns?

They taste "funny."

Why won't the shark eat the overweight diver?

It's trying to eat less fat.

Why won't the shark eat the millionaire?

It's trying to give up rich food.

Why won't the shark eat the garbage collec-
tor?

It's stopped eating "junk food."

What do sharks spread on toast?

"jelly-fish"

What do sharks eat for dessert?

"fish cakes"

What did the shark get when it swallowed a
key ring?

lockjaw

What has fins and sharp teeth, can swim very
fast, and takes care of sick fish?

a nurse shark

Why can you believe everything a shark tells
you?

They're very "tooth-full."

How would you feel if you argued with a shark?

"chewed out"

What would you get if you crossed a blizzard with a shark?

frostbite

Skunks

How can you keep a skunk from smelling?

Hold its nose!

Where do skunks go to college?

"P.U."

Why won't the skunk make the football team?

It's too "pew-ny."

What would you call an argument between skunks?

a "dis-pew-te"

What do you call skunks when they go to school?

"pew-pils"

What did Christopher Robin call his pet skunk?

Winnie-the-"Pew"

What would you get if you crossed a martial arts expert with a skunk?

kung "phew"

What did the bratty little skunk do when it didn't get its own way?

raised a "big stink"

What would you get if you crossed an elephant with a skunk?

a "big stink"

What would you get if you crossed a skunk with an ocean animal?

a "stink-ray"

What did the critic say about the skunk's autobiography?

"It stinks."

What would you get if you crossed a skunk with a big, gray animal that has a trunk?

a "smell-ephant"

What do skunks like to read?

best "smellers"

What's a skunk's favorite candy?

"smelly-beans"

Two raccoons and a skunk sat on a bridge. The raccoons jumped off. Why didn't the skunk?

It had more "scents."

Create new riddles using these patterns.

Snakes

What's a snake's favorite candy?

Hershey's "Hisses"

Why is it hard to fool a snake?

You can't pull its leg.

Why did the snake lose the argument?

It didn't have a leg to stand on.

What would you get if you crossed a kangaroo with a snake?

a jump rope

Where does the snake keep its outgrown skins?

a "shed"

Why don't snakes need silverware?

Their tongues are "forked."

What do snakes like to read?

"hiss-tory" books

What's long, slithers on the ground, and goes "hith, hith"?

a snake with a lisp

Why did the little python give an apple to its teacher?

It had a "crush" on her.

What's very long, crushes its victims, and wears a trench coat and dark glasses?

a "spy-thon"

What slithers on the ground, has sharp fangs, and likes to tell on everybody?

a "tattle-snake"

What slithers on the ground, has sharp fangs, and never stops talking?

a "prattle-snake"

What slithers on the ground, has sharp fangs, and throws tantrums?

a "brat-tlesnake"

What slithers on the ground, has sharp fangs, and is too nervous to think straight?

a "rattled-snake"

What did the baby snake get for its birthday?

a "rattle"

Spiders

See "Creepy Crawlies."

Squirrels

Why do squirrels live in trees?

They can't afford condos.

Where do squirrels store their winter clothes?

in tree "trunks"

What did the squirrel use for building its house?

"wall-nuts"

Who'd want a nutcracker for Christmas?

a toothless squirrel

Where do squirrels go when they want to read books?

"branch" libraries

How do we know that squirrels will take risks?

They'll "go out on a limb."

Tigers

See "Any Animal with Stripes."

Toads

See "Frogs and Toads."

Turtles

What was the turtle doing on the highway?

about one mile per hour

Why do turtles live in shells?

They can't afford apartments.

Why is being a turtle great?

You never have far to walk home.

What's worse off than a giraffe with a sore throat?

> a turtle with claustrophobia

See also Yertle the Turtle and Other Stories *in chapter 8.*

Unicorns

What would you get if you crossed a female sheep with a mythical horned animal?

> a "ewe-nicorn"

What did mythical horned animals eat at summer cookouts?

> "uni-corn on the cob"

Whales

Why did the little whale get in trouble with its mother?

> It "spouted" off.

What whales wear uniforms, tie knots, and go camping?

> Boy "Spouts"

What whales wear green uniforms, go camping, and sell cookies?

> Girl "Spouts"

What do Boy "Spouts" and Girl "Spouts" use to make campfires?

> "fish sticks"

What kind of sandwiches do whales eat?

> "krilled" cheese

What do whales do when they're sad?

> "blubber"

What kinds of whales weigh the least?

> "ba-lean" whales

What are black and white, swim in the ocean, and write suspense novels?

> "thriller" whales

What would you call killer whales that play musical instruments?

> an "orca-stra"

What authors live in the ocean?

> "write" whales

Worms

See "Creepy Crawlies."

Zebras

What has black-and-white stripes and can swing through the trees?

> a "chimpan-zebra"

See also "Any Animal with Stripes."

ZOOS

What do zookeepers put in their soup?

> animal crackers

What's a zookeeper's favorite vegetable?

> "zoo-chini"

Why can't the zoo vet operate on the laughing hyena?

> It's already in "stitches."

Why did caring for the kangaroos wear the zookeeper out?

> They kept her "hopping."

What does the zookeeper use to open the door
to the primate house?
    a "mon-key"

How did the snakes escape from the zoo?
    They "scaled" the walls.

11 "'Hoppy' Birthday!"
Riddles about Birthdays

BIRTHDAYS IN GENERAL

Were any famous men and women born on your birthday?

> no, only little babies

What does the president of the United States always get on his birthday?

> a year older

What goes up but never comes down?

> your age

How did the silly twins try to make time fly the week before their birthday?

> They threw a clock out the window.

When do kangaroos celebrate their birthdays?

> in "leap" year

Why did Humpty Dumpty have a great fall?

> He had a birthday party in October.

BIRTHDAY CARDS AND GREETINGS

Why did the silly kid wrap the birthday card in a scarf before mailing it?

> to send warm wishes

Why didn't the envelope say anything when someone put a birthday card in it and licked its flap?

> It "shut up."

Who sent the pig a birthday card?

> her "pen" pal

How do frogs [or kangaroos or rabbits] greet each other on their birthdays?

> "'Hoppy' Birthday!"

How can you wish a fish a happy birthday?

> Drop it a "line."

How can you wish a slice of bread a happy birthday?

> "Toast" it.

Why didn't the owl wish its friend a happy birthday?

   It didn't give a hoot.

Why did the hummingbird hum while everyone else sang "Happy Birthday"?

   It didn't know the words.

PLANNING THE PARTY

What did the actress have after breaking her leg on her birthday?

   a "cast" party

What do baseball pitchers do on their birthdays?

   "throw" parties

How do soccer players celebrate their birthdays?

   They have a "ball."

Where do geologists celebrate their birthdays?

   "rock" concerts

What do you call kittens who go bowling on their birthdays?

   "alley" cats

Where's the coolest place to hold your birthday party?

   the South Pole

Why won't the farmer tell the pigs about his wife's surprise birthday party?

   They might "squeal."

How did the giant find out about his surprise birthday party?

   Jack "spilled the beans."

Why did the silly kid put lipstick on her forehead before deciding whom to invite to her birthday party?

   to "make up" her mind

Why would it be fun to invite young goats to your birthday party?

   They'd "kid" around.

Why would it be fun to invite surgeons to your birthday party?

   They'd keep you in "stitches."

Why shouldn't you invite pigs to your birthday party?

   They'd "hog" the food.

Why shouldn't you invite turkeys to your birthday party?

   They'd "gobble" the food.

Why don't trees invite the woodpecker to their birthday parties?

   It "bores" them.

Why didn't the hatchet go to the birthday party?

   It wasn't "axed" (asked).

BEFORE THE PARTY

How did the tree prepare for the birthday party?

   It "spruced" up.

What did the dentists use to get to the birthday party on the other side of the river?

   the tooth "ferry"

Why did the silly kids bring dynamite to their friend's birthday party?

   They'd been asked to help "blow up" balloons.

How can you tell when guests have arrived for your birthday party?

You sense their "presents" (presence).

How can you make sure your birthday party starts on time?

Sit on your watch.

PARTY GAMES

Why did the kittens play follow the leader at the birthday party?

They're "copy-cats."

What do librarians play at birthday parties?

follow the "reader"

What do gardeners play at birthday parties?

follow the "weeder"

What do sharks play at birthday parties?

"swallow" the leader

What do groundhogs play at birthday parties?

shadow tag

What do monsters play at birthday parties?

musical "scares"

What do polar bears play at birthday parties?

freeze tag

What do bees play at birthday parties?

"hive"-and-seek

What do young ghosts [or witches] play at birthday parties?

hide-and-"shriek"

What do mice play at birthday parties?

hide-and-"squeak"

Why don't chickens play hide-and-seek at birthday parties?

Someone always "peeps."

Why don't leopards play hide-and-seek at birthday parties?

They're always "spotted."

Why couldn't the ship's crew play cards at the captain's birthday party?

Somebody sat on the "deck."

What rope game do toads play at birthday parties?

tug-of-"warts"

What do tornadoes play at birthday parties?

Twister

ENTERTAINMENT

Why didn't the shark eat the clowns who entertained at its birthday party?

They tasted "funny"!

What did the duck do when the clown entertained at its birthday party?

It "quacked" up.

Why did the teddy bear need mending after the clown act at the birthday party?

It split its sides laughing.

What kind of music do baseball sluggers play at birthday parties?

"hit" songs

DRINKS

What shouldn't you drink around your birthday balloons?

"pop"

What do boxers drink at birthday parties?

"punch"

What do bullies drink at birthday parties?

"Cruel-Aid"

What do cool guys drink at birthday parties?

Mountain "Dude"

What did guests drink at Little Red Riding Hood's birthday party?

"Cloak"-a-Cola

What do sopranos drink at birthday parties?

"High-C"

What kind of cats drink lemonade at birthday parties?

"sour-pusses"

Why did the elephant sit on an ice cube at the birthday party?

It didn't want to fall in the punch.

See also "Fall" in chapter 13. Substitute "drink at birthday parties" for "drink in the fall."

CAKE

Where can you find a really delicious birthday cake?

It depends on where you left it.

What baseball player makes the tastiest birthday cakes?

the best "batter"

What do baseball pitchers enjoy most about making birthday cakes?

licking the "batter"

What did Tinker Bell use to make her friend a birthday cake?

a Peter "pan"

What did the chicken bake for her friend's birthday?

a "layer" cake

What did Lassie put in her birthday cake?

"collie-flour" (cauliflower)

What does Old Man Winter put on top of his birthday cake?

Jack "Frost-ing"

Why couldn't the tennis player light her birthday candles?

She'd lost her "matches."

What should hundred-year-old people do before lighting their birthday candles?

call the fire department

What do basketball players do before blowing out their birthday candles?

make a "swish"

Why will the birthday candles dress up?

They're "going out."

Why won't the teddy bear eat ice cream and cake at the birthday party?

He's already "stuffed."

What's the best thing to put in your birthday cake?

your teeth

What did the polite teeth say to the birthday cake?

"It's a pleasure to 'eat' you."

Why did the silly twins eat their birthday cake on the way home from the bakery?

They came to a "fork" in the road.

What do baseball players use to eat birthday cake?

"pitch-forks"

What do skeletons use for serving ice cream and cake at their birthday parties?

"bone china"

How many pieces of birthday cake can you eat on an empty stomach?

One. After that, your stomach isn't empty.

What kind of birthday cake would you have if you didn't wash your hands before eating it?

"germ 'n'" chocolate (German chocolate)

What do carpenters eat on their birthdays?

"pound" cake

What do deep-sea divers eat on their birthdays?

"sponge" cake

What did Dorothy's cowardly lion friend eat on his birthday?

a "yellow" cake

What do geologists eat on their birthdays?

"marble" cake

What do ghosts in Dallas eat on their birthdays?

Texas "sheet" cake

What do mice eat on their birthdays?

"cheese-cake"

What do rabbits eat on their birthdays?

carrot cake

What do sharks eat on their birthdays?

"fish cakes"

What did the rubber ducky eat on its birthday?

a "cake" of soap

Do monsters eat birthday cake with their fingers?

No. They eat their fingers separately.

What did the leopard say after eating its birthday cake?

"That 'hit the spot.'"

Why did the absentminded professor get heartburn after eating his birthday cake?

He'd forgotten to take off the candles.

What happened when the prisoner ate chocolate cake on his birthday?

He "broke out."

Why will the birthday cake go to the doctor?

It feels "crumb-y."

ICE CREAM

What did Ernie say when his friend asked, "Do you want ice cream with your birthday cake?"

"'Sure, Bert.'"

Why couldn't Mother Goose eat ice cream on her birthday?

Her dish ran away with her spoon.

What did Curious George become after eating a carton of ice cream on his birthday?

a "chunky monkey"

What kind of ice cream do ghosts eat on their birthdays?

"boo-berry"

What kind of ice cream do sea monsters eat on their birthdays?

chocolate "ship"

What do witches eat at birthday parties?

ice "scream" and cake

What do cats eat at birthday parties?

"mice" cream and cake

Why are guests disgusted about having to eat ice cream and cake in the birthday girl's tree house?

They're "fed up."

OTHER KINDS OF REFRESHMENTS

What do garbage collectors eat at birthday parties?

"junk" food

What do he-men eat at birthday parties?

"machos" and cheese

Why does Goldilocks like the refreshments at Baby Bear's birthday party?

They're just right.

PRESENTS

What did the birthday gift say when the teacher took attendance?

"Present."

Why don't oysters give each other birthday presents?

They're "shellfish."

Why do mummies make good birthday presents?

They're gift wrapped.

What's a silly thing to give a kangaroo on its birthday?

a trampoline

What's the world's most useless birthday present?

a solar-powered flashlight

Why did the silly aunt give her nephew three socks for his birthday?

She heard he'd grown another "foot."

What did the baby snake get for its birthday?

a "rattle"

What did the boy say when he put his watch in the remote-controlled airplane he got for his birthday?

"Time flies when you're having fun."

What did the bald man say when he got a comb for his birthday?

"I'll never part with it."

What did the rude skunk say when it got a birthday present it didn't like?

"It stinks!"

What would happen if you spent all of your birthday money on candy?

You'd put your money where your mouth is.

AFTER THE PARTY

How did the skeleton feel after its all-day
birthday party?

"bone tired"

Why did the vacuum cleaner resent the
mother who was cleaning up after her child's
birthday party?

She pushed it around.

Why do you have to go to bed at the end of
your birthday?

Your bed won't come to you.

12 Frightfully Funny

*Riddles about
Creepy Creatures*

GHOSTS

How do ghosts amuse themselves around a campfire?

> They tell people stories.

What authors make up the scariest stories?

> "ghost-writers"

Why is it easy to have ghosts spend the night?

> They bring their own sheets.

Why can't you tell when a ghost feels faint?

> It's always white as a sheet.

When do ghosts appear?

> just before somebody screams

What do actors get if they see a ghost?

> stage fright

What happened when the horse saw a ghost?

> It "spooked."

What would you have if a ghost moved into your closet?

> "scaredy-pants"

What would you call it if you got a computer message from a ghost?

> "eek!-mail"

What time of year do ghosts like best?

> the dead of winter

What game do little ghosts play with their friends?

> hide-and-"shriek"

How can you get in a haunted house when the door is locked?

> Use a "spook-key."

What do ghosts do during baseball games?

> "boo" the umpire

Why did the little ghost ask the school nurse for a Band-Aid?

It had a "boo-boo."

What do baby ghosts play with their parents?

"shriek-a-boo"

Who blows a horn, sleeps under a haystack, and haunts Mother Goose?

Little Boy "Boo!"

What kind of pants do ghosts wear?

"boo!" jeans

Create new riddles using "boo" instead of "blue."

Why were the silly kids scared when their teacher talked about school spirit?

They thought the school was haunted.

What do the [name a team] call the ghost in their locker room?

the team "spirit"

What ghost wears a red hat and says, "Ho, ho, ho"?

the Christmas "spirit"

What do you call ghosts that haunt skyscrapers?

high "spirits"

Why don't ghosts like to go out in the rain?

It dampens their "spirits."

Why do ghosts enjoy riding in elevators?

It lifts their "spirits."

What was the ghost family's motto?

"Scare and scare alike."

What storybook character do ghosts like best?

"Ra-moan-a" Quimby

See also the reproducible riddles for ghost puppets in appendix C.

MUMMIES

What did King Tut grow in his flower garden?

"chrysanthe-mummies"

What do mummies talk about?

old times

Why can't the mummy answer the phone?

It's "tied up."

Why are mummies always late?

They get "tied up."

How do mummy [name any sport] games always end?

in a "tie"

What do mummies use to disguise themselves?

"mask-ing" tape

What happened when the little mummy got into trouble?

It was sent to its "tomb."

Why are mummies always tense?

They never "unwind."

Why do mummies enjoy their jobs?

They're "wrapped up" in their work.

Why don't mummies make good friends?

They're "wrapped up" in themselves.

Why do mummies make good spies?

They keep things under "wraps."

What did the mummy detective say when it solved the mystery?

> "That 'wraps' up the case."

What happened when the mummy got a really bad cold?

> It couldn't stop "coffin."

VAMPIRES

Why did the little vampire get in trouble at school?

> He had a "bat" attitude.

What happened when the vampire forgot to brush his teeth?

> He got "bat" breath.

What do vampires wear over their pajamas?

> "bat-robes"

Create new riddles using the word "bat."

What will the vampire do at the track meet?

> grab a quick "bite"

What would you get if you crossed the Abominable Snowman with a vampire?

> frostbite

Why doesn't the actress in the horror movie like her role as the vampire's victim?

> It's a "bit" part.

Why do vampires drink blood?

> Root beer makes them burp.

How do we know that vampires are very competitive?

> They're always out for blood.

What did the vampire do in art class?

> He "drew" blood.

What do little vampires study for in school?

> "blood tests"

What would you get if you crossed a vampire with a beagle?

> a bloodhound

What would you get if you crossed a vampire with a car?

> a bloodmobile

What would you get if you crossed a vampire with a credit union?

> a "blood bank"

What did the vampire do at the blood bank?

> He made a withdrawal.

What happened when the vampire got a really bad cold?

> He couldn't stop "coffin."

How are vampires like false teeth?

> They come out at night.

Why do vampires sleep all day?

> Who wants to wake them up?

WEREWOLVES

What happened when the werewolf read a riddle book?

> It "howled" with laughter.

Why do readers laugh at the book about werewolves?

> It's a "howl."

What's hairy and scary and uses bad language [or profanity]?

a "swear-wolf"

What's hairy and scary and keeps its eye out for danger?

a "beware-wolf"

Who's a student at Hogwarts, plays Quidditch, and turns into a werewolf when the moon is full?

"Hairy" Potter

Who helped the werewolf go to the ball?

its "hairy" godmother

WITCHES

What do you call someone who takes care of sick sorceresses?

witch doctors

Why do witches fly on brooms?

Vacuum cleaner cords are too short.

What happened when the witch flew her broomstick through the car wash?

She made a "clean sweep."

What do witches ask for [or request] when they stay in hotels?

"broom" service

What do witches in Australia ride?

"broom-erangs"

Why don't witches ride their brooms when they're angry?

They might fly off the handle.

What do witches wear on their wrists?

"charmed" bracelets

What do witches eat for breakfast?

"Scream" of Wheat

What do witches put on bagels?

"scream" cheese

What do witches eat at birthday parties?

ice "scream" and cake

What did the bat tell the witch's hat?

"You go on 'a head.' I'll 'hang around' here."

Where do witches have their hair done?

ugly parlors

Why do witches wear green eye shadow?

It matches their teeth.

How do witches keep in shape?

They "hex-ercise."

What time is it when a witch turns a prince into a frog?

"spring-time"

What do tired witches do?

They rest a "spell."

Who casts spells at the haunted beach?

"sand-witches"

See also "Ghosts," substituting "witches" for "ghosts" when "shriek" is part of the answer, as well as "Harry Potter Series" in chapter 8, substituting "witch" for "Harry Potter" when the answer involves spells.

13 "'Hoppy' Holidays!"
Riddles about Holidays and Seasons

NEW YEAR'S DAY

What always needs changing on January 1st?
> Baby New Year

What do caterpillars do on January 1st?
> turn over a new leaf

How can you make sure you'll stick to your list of New Year's resolutions?
> Pour glue on it.

How are New Year's resolutions like eggs?
> They're easy to break.

Why did the [name a geometric shape] resolve to exercise more in the coming year?
> to get in "shape"

How do frogs greet each other on January 1st?
> "'Hoppy' New Year!"

How do reporters greet each other on January 1st?
> "Happy 'News' Year!"

How do amphibians greet each other on January 1st?
> "Happy 'Newt' Year!"

How do cows greet each other on January 1st?
> "Happy 'Moo' Year!"

Create new riddles using words that rhyme with "new."

What do gardeners use for arranging flowers on New Year's Day?
> a rose bowl

CHINESE NEW YEAR

When can a monkey turn into a rooster?
> at Chinese New Year

Adapt this by finding out what the current year is and what the new year will be. See www .chinapage.com/newyear.html for exact dates, which vary from January 21 to February 21.

GROUNDHOG DAY

Why did the brave groundhog mess up the weather predictions?

> It wasn't afraid of its shadow.

What game do groundhogs play on February 2nd?

> shadow tag

What would you call a young woodchuck whose parents won't let him leave his burrow?

> a "grounded-hog"

What would you call Charlie Brown if he became a lumberjack?

> a "wood-Chuck"

What would you call a groundhog that refused to look for its shadow on February 2nd?

> a "wouldn't-chuck"

VALENTINE'S DAY

What do you call a very small card for February 14th?

> a "valen-tiny"

Why should you open your valentines quickly?

> to get to the "heart" of the matter

What happened when Dorothy sent the witch a warm and loving valentine?

> She melted her heart.

What happened when the girl left her chocolate valentine on top of the stove?

> It melted her heart.

Why did the boy give giant valentines to everyone on February 14th?

> He's "big-hearted."

Why did the boy stick his valentines in the freezer?

> He's "cold-hearted."

Why did the girl wrap her valentines in a scarf?

> She's "warm-hearted."

Why did the girl paint Valentine's Day messages on rocks?

> She's "hard-hearted."

Why did the boy write Valentine's Day messages on marshmallows?

> He's "tender-hearted."

How did the girl feel when she accidentally dropped the glass valentine her boyfriend gave her?

> "broken-hearted"

What would you get if you accidentally spilled sugar on your valentines?

> "sweet-hearts"

How do two valentines talk?

> "heart to heart"

How did the bat feel when the baseball player gave it a sentimental valentine?

> all "choked up"

Why did the girl python give the boy python a valentine?

> She had a "crush" on him.

Why did the apple give a valentine to the orange?

> It had an "Orange Crush."

Who gave the bird a dozen red roses on Valentine's Day?

> her "tweet-heart"

Who gave the pig a fancy heart-shaped box of chocolates on February 14th?

> her "valen-swine"

Who gave the piece of string a fancy card on February 14th?

> her "valen-twine"

What did the caveman give his wife on Valentine's Day?

> "rock candy"

What did the tomcat give his girlfriend on Valentine's Day?

> "purr-fume"

What do pandas give each other on Valentine's Day?

> bear hugs

Where does Robin Hood buy roses for Maid Marian on Valentine's Day?

> Sherwood "Florist"

Why do skunks enjoy Valentine's Day?

> They're "scent-imental."

LEAP DAY

When are most kangaroos born?

> leap year

What would you get if you crossed a frog with a calendar?

> leap year

What would you get if you crossed the sandman with a calendar?

> "sleep" year

DR. SEUSS'S BIRTHDAY (MARCH 2ND)

See chapter 8 for riddles about Dr. Seuss's books and chapter 11 for birthday riddles you can adapt.

ST. PATRICK'S DAY

What's green and Irish and sits on your porch every March 17th?

> "Paddy O' Furniture"

What holiday do flying mammals celebrate on March 17th?

> St. "Bat-rick's" Day

What do leprechauns call artificial stones?

> "sham-rocks"

What kind of music do leprechauns like?

> "sham-rock"

What would you get if you crossed a leprechaun with a purple dinosaur?

> "Blarney"

Why don't leprechauns form a baseball team?

They'd have too many "short-stops."

Why do leprechauns always hurry?

They're "short" of time.

How does the leprechaun feel after running a mile?

"short" of breath

Why are the leprechauns behind in their work?

They're "short-handed."

Why do leprechauns keep borrowing money?

They're always "short."

What did the leprechaun call his autobiography?

A "Short" Story

What do leprechauns like to read?

"short" stories

What's a leprechaun's favorite dessert?

strawberry "short-cake"

What kind of Girl Scout cookies do leprechauns buy?

"short-bread"

What do you call a conversation between leprechauns?

"small talk"

Where do leprechauns play baseball?

in the "Little League"

What kind of seafood do leprechauns like?

shrimp

SPRING

What season is it when you play on a trampoline?

"spring"

What time is it when a witch turns a prince into a frog?

"spring-time"

Why did the mattress go to Florida?

for "spring" training

What did the mattress have when it ran a temperature?

"spring" fever

What happened when the bedbugs fell in love?

They got married in the "spring."

What did March say to February when the waiter brought their dinner check?

"I'll 'spring' for it."

APRIL FOOLS' DAY

What storybook scientist played April Fools' Day jokes on his monster?

Dr. "Prank-enstein"

What famous American enjoyed playing April Fools' Day jokes on the other Founding Fathers?

Benjamin "Prank-lin"

What happened when all the king's men played an April Fools' Day joke on Humpty Dumpty?

He "fell for it."

How can you play an April Fools' Day joke on a sheep?

Pull the wool over its eyes.

Why is it hard to play an April Fools' Day joke on a snake?

You can't pull its leg.

Why do seabirds always fall for April Fools' Day jokes?

They're "gull-ible."

EASTER

What sport does the Easter Bunny play?

"basket-ball"

What does the Easter Bunny put on his peanut butter sandwiches?

"jelly-beans"

What did the Easter Bunny have after getting up on the wrong side of the bed?

a bad "hare" day

What does the Easter Bunny call his factory?

an "egg-plant"

How many colored eggs can the Easter Bunny put into an empty basket that's twelve inches long, five inches tall, and six inches deep?

One. After that, it's not empty.

Where did the Easter Bunny get off the highway?

the "eggs-it"

How can you tell where the Easter Bunny's been?

"Eggs" mark the spot.

Who delivers colored eggs and candy to tadpoles each spring?

the Easter "Ribbit"

What would you get if you crossed a baby chick with the Easter Bunny?

"Peeper" Cottontail

How did the silly farmers try to get colored Easter eggs?

They fed their hens crayons.

Why do people paint Easter eggs?

Wallpaper doesn't fit.

What do members of the orchestra eat on Easter?

"harp-boiled" eggs

What Easter eggs are cowardly?

the "yellow" ones

What should you do with a blue Easter egg?

Cheer it up.

Where does the Easter Bunny get blue eggs?

sad chickens

What kind of candy do skunks get in their Easter baskets?

"smelly-beans"

What did Jack get after planting his Easter candy?

a "jellybean-stalk"

Where's the best place to hide your Easter candy?

in your mouth

Where did the police put the chocolate bunny that stole Easter baskets?

    behind candy "bars"

What do antelopes get for Easter?

    "gnu" clothes

NATIONAL LIBRARY WEEK

National Library Week is generally the second full week in April; for exact dates, check the website for the American Library Association at www.ala.org/ ala/pio/natlibraryweek/nlw.cfm. For appropriate riddles, see "Libraries" in chapter 7.

D.E.A.R. DAY (APRIL 12TH)

Who doesn't like when it's time to Drop Everything and Read (D.E.A.R.)?

    the owner of a china shop

For more riddles, see "Ramona Series" in chapter 8. For information about D.E.A.R. Day, visit its website at www.dropeverythingandread.com.

CHILDREN'S BOOK WEEK

Children's Book Week is the first or second week of May; for exact dates, check the website for the Children's Book Council at www.cbcbooks.org. For appropriate riddles, see chapter 7.

SUMMER

What did summer say to spring?

    "Help! I'm going to 'fall'!"

What did the surfers do when the temperature hit 100 degrees?

    They caught a heat "wave."

What do chickens lay during heat waves?

    hard-boiled eggs

What did the witch do when she got tired of the heat wave?

    She cast a cold "spell."

How is a puppy on a summer day like something you eat at a baseball game?

    It's a "hot dog."

Who brought the alligator a cold drink on a hot day?

    its "Gator-aide"

What do bullies drink on hot summer days?

    "Cruel-Aid"

What do really popular kids drink on hot summer days?

    "Cool-Aid"

What do cats drink on hot summer days?

    "mice" tea

What do cats put in lemonade on hot summer days?

    "mice" cubes

Why will reading ghost stories help you cool off on hot summer days?

    They're "chilling."

What helps authors [or movie stars or sports stars] cool off on hot summer days?

    reading "fan" mail

What keeps rabbits cool when the weather gets hot?

    "hare-conditioning"

What goes "ouch, ouch, ouch, ouch, ouch, ouch, ouch, ouch"?

> a spider crossing a hot sidewalk

What do spiders eat at summer cookouts?

> corn on the "cob-web"

What did mythical horned animals eat at summer cookouts?

> "uni-corn on the cob"

What do gymnasts put on corn on the cob in July and August?

> "somersault" (summer salt)

What will you get if you eat too much corn on the cob at your summer cookout?

> an "ear-ache"

What's worse than having it rain cats and dogs during your summer cookout?

> having it "hail" taxis

What do young sorceresses make at summer camp?

> "witch-crafts"

What animal is gray and has a trunk?

> a mouse on summer vacation

What do you call a rodent that's getting ready to go on vacation?

> a "pack" rat

What did the boxer pack when he went on vacation?

> punching bags

What did the squirrel pack when it went on vacation?

> its tree "trunk"

How can you learn about hotels and motels before you go on vacation?

> Search the "Inn-ternet."

Where do cats go when they take a vacation?

> "Ber-mew-da"

Where do pet birds go when they take a vacation?

> the Canary Islands

Where do eye doctors go when they take a vacation?

> the "see-shore"

Where does Santa stay when he goes on vacation?

> a "ho-ho-hotel"

What did the bread do on its summer vacation?

> "loafed" around

How can you make meat loaf?

> Send it on summer vacation.

Why can't basketball players ever go on vacation?

> They're not allowed to "travel."

Why didn't the skeleton go away on vacation?

> It had "no body" to go with.

FOURTH OF JULY

Why does the Statue of Liberty stand in New York Harbor?

> She can't sit down.

What happened when one of our Founding Fathers told a joke near the Liberty Bell?

> It "cracked" up.

Why do firecrackers look forward to the Fourth of July?

They get a "bang" out of it.

What does Polly the parrot want on the Fourth of July?

a "fire-cracker"

What did the silly kid put in his soup on the Fourth of July?

"fire-crackers"

What do ducks light on the Fourth of July?

"fire-quackers"

What's the best thing to drink when you're setting off firecrackers?

"pop"

What makes more noise than a firecracker on the Fourth of July?

two firecrackers on the Fourth of July

What happened when Humpty Dumpty set off firecrackers on the wall?

He fell down and went boom.

Why do stores that sell fireworks make lots of money on the Fourth of July?

Business is "booming."

HARRY POTTER'S BIRTHDAY (JULY 31ST)

See "Harry Potter Series" in chapter 8.

LIBRARY CARD SIGN-UP MONTH (SEPTEMBER)

See "Libraries" in chapter 7.

FALL

What season do gymnasts like least? [Or use these: What season's most like Humpty Dumpty? What's the worst time of year for skateboarding? What's the best time of year for skydiving?]

fall

When is a book like a tree in the fall?

when its "leaves" are turning

How were cattle thieves in the Old West like autumn leaves?

They "rustled."

Why is the maple leaf afraid to fall off the tree?

It's "yellow."

Why did the leaf end up in the emergency room?

It had a bad fall.

Why does the silly kid lay pillows under the trees every autumn?

to cushion the leaves' fall

Why couldn't the tennis player burn her leaves in the fall?

She'd lost her "matches."

Why did Humpty Dumpty have a great fall?

to make up for a miserable summer

What do computer programmers drink in the fall?

apple "cyber"

What do baseball players drink in the fall?

apple "slider"

What do frogs and toads drink in the fall?

apple "spider"

What do secret agents drink in the fall?

apple "spy-der"

What did the maiden's true love give her on the last day of fall?

a partridge in a "bare" tree

HALLOWEEN

What would you have if the Easter Bunny showed up on October 31st?

a "hoppy" Halloween

Why is Halloween a happy holiday?

It's when "spirits" rise.

Why does the turkey wear the same Halloween costume every year?

It's always "a-gobblin'" (a goblin).

What do mummies wear to Halloween parties?

"mask-ing" tape

Who casts spells at the beach on Halloween?

"sand-witches"

What's fun to roast around a bonfire on October 31st?

"Hallo-wieners"

What do computer programmers do at Halloween parties?

bob for "Apples"

What did the doctor say on Halloween?

"Trick or 'treat-ment'!"

What do canaries say on Halloween?

"Trick or 'tweet'!"

What did the snake give out on Halloween?

Hershey's "Hisses"

What did Snow White's prince give out on Halloween?

Hershey's Kisses

What did the beaver give out on Halloween?

"Tree" Musketeers bars

Where's the best place to hide your Halloween candy?

in your mouth

See also chapter 12 and the pumpkin bookmark in appendix C.

THANKSGIVING

What do aquariums celebrate on the fourth Thursday in November?

"Tanks-giving"

Who wrote *The Pilgrims' Voyage*?

May Flower

If April showers bring May flowers, what do May flowers bring?

Pilgrims

Why did the Pilgrims cross the ocean in the *Mayflower*?

It was too far to swim.

How did the Pilgrims sleep on the *Mayflower*?

They closed their eyes.

What kind of vegetables didn't the Pilgrims want on the *Mayflower*?

"leeks"

What kind of music did the Pilgrims enjoy?

Plymouth "rock"

What do you call your Thanksgiving turkey when it's still in the freezer?

a "brrr-d"

Why did the silly cook have trouble dressing her Thanksgiving turkey?

She couldn't find clothes that fit.

What's the best way to stuff a turkey on Thanksgiving?

Feed it plenty of pizza.

Who's never hungry for Thanksgiving dinner?

The turkey's already "stuffed."

What did the referee call the basketball player's Thanksgiving turkey?

a personal "fowl"

Where does the catcher sit during the baseball team's Thanksgiving dinner?

behind the "plate"

What will quarterbacks do during Thanksgiving dinner?

"pass" the turkey

What did the rock band bring to the Thanksgiving potluck?

"drumsticks"

What would you get if you crossed a turkey with an octopus?

plenty of drumsticks on Thanksgiving

Why is the salad hiding behind the Thanksgiving turkey?

It's "dressing."

What do geometry teachers eat for dessert on Thanksgiving?

pumpkin "pi"

Where should you bury the bones after Thanksgiving dinner?

a "gravy-yard"

HANUKKAH

What Hanukkah game is really boring?

"drei-dull"

What would you get if you crossed a dreidel with the storybook puppet that came to life?

"Spin-occhio"

What would you get if you crossed Mickey Mouse's creator with a spinning dreidel?

Walt "Dizzy"

What did one dreidel say to the other dreidel?

"We must be lost. We keep going in circles."

Why will the Hanukkah candles dress up?

They're "going out."

WINTER

What time of year do ghosts like best?

the dead of winter

How can you learn more about the coldest season of the year?

Search the "Winter-net."

What does Old Man Winter put on his birth-day cake?

"Jack Frost-ing"

What falls in winter but never lands on the ground?

the temperature

Why did the thermometer break?

The temperature dropped.

What has no teeth but still can bite?

the cold

Why do skeletons hate winter?

The cold goes right through them.

What would you get if your father shoveled snow without wearing a coat?

ice-cold "Pop"

What keeps evergreen trees warm all winter?

"fir" (fur) coats

What keeps houses warm all winter?

"coats" of paint

Where do squirrels store their winter clothes?

in tree "trunks"

Why do birds fly south for the winter?

It's too far to walk.

Why do bears sleep all winter?

They can't afford alarm clocks.

What do you call it when a bear sleeps in a treetop all winter?

"high-bernation"

Where can you always find tracks in winter?

railroad stations

Why shouldn't you buy snow tires for your car on sunny days?

They'll melt before you get home.

What happens when you wear snowshoes?

You get cold feet.

What do you call pavement that's covered with ice?

a "slide-walk"

See also various winter sports in chapter 14 and "Snow" in chapter 16.

CHRISTMAS

What ghost wears a red hat and says, "Ho, ho, ho"?

the Christmas "spirit"

How do frogs [or kangaroos or rabbits] greet each other in December?

"'Hoppy' Holidays!"

What would you get if you accidentally spilled salt and pepper on your Christmas cards?

"seasoned" greetings

What do you call an insect that can't stand Christmas?

"Hum-bug!"

How did the clock [or mummy] feel on Christmas Eve?

all "wound up"

What do astronauts hang in their doorways at Christmas?

"missile-toe"

Why do the Christmas tree lights need to visit the eye doctor?

They're on the "blink."

What Christmas tree is always sad?

a "blue" spruce

Why did Ebenezer Scrooge like finding coal in his stocking on Christmas morning?

It saved on heat.

What has antlers, lives in Africa, and delivers presents on Christmas Eve?

"Santa-lope"

What's furry, says "meow," and delivers presents on Christmas Eve?

Santa "Claws"

How can you tell if Santa has come?

You sense his "presents" (presence).

What does Santa call his figurines?

"St. Nick-knacks"

What would you call Santa if he cut himself shaving?

St. "Nicked"

What would you call Santa if he played basketball for New York City?

St. "Knick"

Why do reindeer pull Santa's sleigh?

Elephants would crash through the roof.

What would you get if you crossed a storm cloud with Rudolph?

a "rain-deer"

When does Santa need an umbrella?

when "rain-deer" fly overhead

Which of Santa's reindeer has a bright red nose?

the one with a very bad cold

What's the first thing Santa does when he gets in his sleigh?

He sits down.

What does Santa tell his reindeer when they land on a roof?

"Whoa!"

Where does Santa go after delivering the last Christmas present?

ho-ho-home

What does Santa Claus do when he works in his garden?

He "hoe-hoe-hoes."

Create new riddles using words that start with "ho."

What does Santa use for catching fish?

the North "Pole"

Why does the martial arts instructor admire Santa?

He has a black belt.

What did Santa's elf need after twisting her ankle?

a candy "cane"

What's a nice treat to give to the person who repairs your sink on Christmas Day?

"plumber" pudding

What ballerina ate too much Christmas candy?

the Sugar "Plump" Fairy

Where do dancers keep their money while performing in the *Nutcracker*?

the "Vaults" of the Flowers

Why do the little lamb and the girl it follows enjoy December every year?

They always have a "Mary" Christmas.

Why does music fill the library at Christmas-time?

Lewis "Carrolls"

How do stockings celebrate Christmas?

They "hang around."

See also riddles about cards and presents in chapter 11, substituting "Christmas" for "birthday" where appropriate.

KWANZAA

What did the black candles in the kinara say to the red and green candles in the kinara?

"Let's go out tonight!"

What would you get if you crossed an African American holiday with Harry Potter's magic stick?

"Kwand-zaa"

NEW YEAR'S EVE

What do people make on New Year's Eve that no one can see?

lots of noise

How do cows make noise on New Year's Eve?

They blow their horns.

When will Mother Goose ask Little Boy Blue to blow his horn?

on New Year's Eve

See also party riddles in chapter 11, substituting "New Year's Eve" for "birthday" where appropriate.

14 Fun(ny) and Games
Riddles about Sports

ANY SPORT

Fill in the blanks with the name of a sport.

Why was Cinderella a lousy _____ player?

    She had a pumpkin for a coach.

Why did Cinderella get kicked off the _____ team?

    She kept running away from the ball.

Why do _____ teams want Snow White to referee their games?

    She's the "fairest" one of all.

What would you get if you crossed a _____ player with an automobile?

    a "sports" car

Who plays _____ in your living room?

    the "home" team

How did the chicken feel after playing _____?

    "eggs-hausted"

What did the _____ players call the ghost in their locker room?

    the team "spirit"

What happened when the [name a team] played the monsters' team?

    They got eaten alive!

How are winning _____ teams like fried eggs?

    They can't be beat.

How are losing _____ teams like scrambled eggs?

    They're always beaten.

Why don't players on losing _____ teams ever get sick?

    They never "catch" anything.

Why are the _____ players all dressed up?

It's a "tie" game.

What did the silly _____ player do when the coach called time out?

He threw his watch off the _____.

(For example: What did the silly basketball player do when the coach called time out?

He threw his watch off the court.)

What did the silly _____ players do when the coach told them to warm the bench?

They spread blankets on it.

BASEBALL

Where do people play baseball underground?

the "miner" leagues

What army officer also plays professional baseball?

"Major" Leaguer

What do you call a baseball stadium when the home team loses?

a "bawl" park

When do baseball players wear armor?

"knight" games

Why did players know exactly what to do after their coach spread blankets across the ball diamond?

He'd "covered" all the bases.

What did the baseball umpire say when the clock made three strikes?

"Time out!"

Why did the outfielder catch a lot of flies during the World Series?

He had a "frog" in his throat.

Why did the outfielder have the sniffles?

He'd "caught" a cold.

Why does the outfielder wear bright, colorful clothes when she's not playing baseball?

to "catch" the eye

What did the orchestra's baseball team use for home plate?

a "base" drum

How did the bat feel when the baseball player gave it a sentimental valentine?

all "choked up"

Why did the baseball player need the Heimlich maneuver?

She was "choking" on the bat.

Why has the baseball slugger made a lot of money on the song he recorded?

It's a "hit."

What do baseball pitchers enjoy most about making cakes?

licking the "batter"

What did Mickey Mouse's friend do when he saw a stray baseball coming right at him?

Donald ducked.

Why did the panty hose win the baseball game?

They got a "run."

Why did the umpire kick the angry pitcher out of the game?

He'd "thrown" a fit.

Why wasn't the prince allowed to pitch for Cinderella's baseball team?

He threw too many "balls."

BASKETBALL

Why do basketball players need bibs to eat soup?

They "dribble."

What would you get if you crossed a kangaroo with a basketball player?

a "jump" shot

Why can't basketball players ever go on vacation?

They're not allowed to "travel."

What's a cheapskate's favorite part of playing basketball?

getting "free" throws

What do basketball players put on their sandwiches?

"swish" cheese

What do basketball players do at breakfast?

"dunk" doughnuts

How did the silly hoops player sink the ball?

He threw it in the lake.

What did the circus dog do at the basketball game?

It jumped through the hoops.

Why will the basketball referee blow the whistle on the tired kangaroo?

It's out of "bounds."

BOXING

Why is the boxer drinking lots of fluids and getting plenty of rest?

to "fight" a cold

What do boxers do the night before a test?

"hit" the books

Why has the boxer made a lot of money on the song he recorded?

It's a "hit."

What do you call a banana that boxes?

a fruit "punch"

Why did the stand-up comedian hire boxers to form a row behind her onstage?

She needed a "punch" line.

Why did the tenderhearted fighter strap pillows around his boxing gloves?

to soften his blows

Why did the boxer want to fight the ice-cream cone?

He knew he could "lick" it.

What did the badly defeated boxer put on his pie?

"whipped" cream

What did the badly defeated boxer spread on his crackers?

"creamed" cheese

How did the boxing match between artists end?

in a "draw"

CAR RACING AND DEMOLITION DERBY

Why did the turkey become a race car driver?

to prove it wasn't a "chicken"

What do race car drivers eat?

fast food

Why is the race car driver tired of his job?

It's a "drag."

How do we know the truck towing the race car is sneaky?

It's "pulling a fast one."

What do demolition derby drivers eat with gravy?

"smashed" potatoes

DOGSLED RACING

What do sled dogs get for winning races?

"cold" medals

What did the driver feed his sled dogs?

"Mush!"

FOOTBALL

What's yellow with black stripes, makes honey, and drops the football all the time?

the "fumble-bee"

Where do ants play football?

in a "sugar bowl"

Where do gardeners play football?

in the Rose Bowl

What do quarterbacks do in the forest?

take a "hike"

Why does the quarterback say "Hike" when logging on to his computer?

That's his "pass-word."

Why did the quarterback need first aid?

He'd "passed" out.

Why did the quarterback toss a wristwatch to his teammates before the game started?

to "pass" the time

Why did the silly football player throw fishing gear at the quarterback?

to "tackle" him

Why did the silly football player carry a garbage bag onto the field?

to "sack" the quarterback

What did the silly football player do when the coach said to go deep?

He went scuba diving.

What happened when the eggs played football?

The game turned into a "scramble."

Why do footballs enjoy being footballs?

They get a "kick" out of it.

What do footballs get from players who take good care of themselves?

a health "kick"

How can you keep a mule from kicking?

Take away its football.

GYMNASTICS

What sport appeals to people named James?

"Jim-nastics"

Why did Jack and Jill win a blue ribbon at the gymnastics meet?

They're good at "tumbling."

Who won the gymnastics meet held in the desert?

the "tumble-weed"

What do you call gymnasts who turn somersaults so quickly they're hard to see?

"tum-blurs"

How do gymnasts decide which team will go first in a meet?

They "flip" for it.

Why did the gymnast carry her checkbook when she performed on the beam?

to keep her "balance"

ICE HOCKEY AND SKATING

What did Ebenezer Scrooge wear to play ice hockey?

"cheap-skates"

What do chickens wear to play ice hockey?

"cheep-skates"

What do Mickey and Minnie wear to play ice hockey?

"mice" skates

Why did the magicians win the hockey championship?

They're good at "hat tricks."

How did the hockey player make friends with the swimmer?

She "broke the ice."

Why shouldn't skaters [or name a skater] tell jokes to the ice?

It might "crack up."

Where do figure skaters swim?

"twirl-pools"

IN-LINE SKATING

What sport is just right for Madeline and her friends?

in-line skating

What's the hardest thing about learning to in-line skate?

the pavement

What would you call Ebenezer Scrooge's Rollerblades?

"cheap-skates"

What would you call a chicken's Rollerblades?

"cheep-skates"

What would you call Mickey's and Minnie's Rollerblades?

"mice" skates

MARTIAL ARTS

What did the karate expert call her paintings?

"martial art"

What martial art do bakers practice?

"ju-dough" and tae kwon "dough"

What martial art requires formal dress?

"tie" kwon do

Why does the martial arts instructor admire Santa?

He has a black belt.

What did the farmer get when her pig took karate lessons?

pork "chops"

What did the shepherd get when his sheep took karate lessons?

lamb "chops"

SKATEBOARDING

What do you call a Rollerblade with nothing to do?

a "skate-bored"

Why did the chicken buy a skateboard?

It liked "eggs-treme" sports.

Why did the turkey go skateboarding?

to prove it wasn't a "chicken"

Why don't centipedes ride skateboards?

They can't afford knee pads.

What did the cats say when they saw mice go by on skateboards?

"Look! Meals on Wheels!"

SNOWBOARDING

What winter sport is terribly dull?

"snow-bored-ing"

SOCCER

Why did the grass have to leave the soccer team?

It was "cut."

How do soccer players solve problems?

They use their heads.

Why did the silly soccer player have trouble eating a popcorn ball?

She thought she couldn't use her hands.

See also "Football," substituting "soccer ball" for "football."

SWIMMING

Where do ballerinas swim?

"twirl-pools"

Where do automobiles swim?

"car-pools"

What happened when the silly kid carried a bowl of salsa to the Y?

He took a "dip" in the pool.

What do teachers do before they swim?

"test" the water

Why did the turkey jump off the high dive?

to prove it wasn't a "chicken"

See also "Sports" in chapter 15.

15 Talking Turnips

Riddles for Talking Turnip Bulletin Boards, Games, and Story

Use these riddles by themselves or with the bulletin boards in chapter 1, the games in chapter 3, and the folktale in appendix A. (See the cards in appendix C for more riddles about objects that talk.)

ANIMALS

What did the antelope say when it heard the latest gossip?

"That's 'gnus' to me."

What did the polite cat say when it met a mouse?

"It's a pleasure to 'eat' you."

What did the cow say to her calf one night?

"It's 'pasture' bedtime. Go to sleep."

What did one cow say to the other cow?

"What's 'moo' with you?"

How do polite cows greet each other?

"How do you 'moo'?"

How do polite doves greet each other?

"How do you 'coo'?"

What did the mother firefly ask at the parent-teacher conference?

"Is my child 'bright'?"

What do fireflies say at the start of a race?

"Ready, set, 'glow'!"

What did the firefly on guard duty say?

"Who 'glows' there?"

What did the angry hen say to the farmer?

"I'm tired of working for chicken feed."

What did the hen say when it laid a square egg?

"Ouch!"

What did the horse say as it finished its meal?

"This is the last straw."

What did one sleepy horse say to the other sleepy horse?

"Let's hit the hay."

What did the mouse pilot say to the passengers?

"This is your captain 'squeaking.'"

What did the rabbit say when the teacher took attendance?

"'Ear' I am."

What do rabbits say when they're calling on friends?

"Is 'any-bunny' home?"

What did one female sheep say when it agreed with the other female sheep?

"'Ewe' said it!"

AROUND THE HOUSE

What did the bossy battery say to the other batteries?

"I'll take 'charge.'"

What did the big candle say to the small candle?

"You're too little to go out at night."

What did the checkerboard say when it was asked to try something new?

"I'm 'game.'"

What did the big chimney say to the little chimney?

"You're too young to smoke."

What did one clock say to the other clock?

"Can you give me a hand?"

What did the big hand on the clock say to the little hand?

"I'll be back in an hour."

What did the mother clock tell her shy son?

"Take your hands off your face."

What did the computer ask the computer programmer?

"Please close my 'Windows.' It's cold in here."

What did the computer say to the virus?

"Quit 'bugging' me."

What did one plate in the cafeteria say to the other plate in the cafeteria?

"'Lunch is on me.'"

What did the tired dishcloth say to the sink?

"I'm 'wiped out.'"

What did the carefree lamp say to the overly serious lamp?

"'Lighten up.'"

What did one match say to the other match?

"I'm 'burned out.'"

What did the matchbook say to the match?

"Are you trying to start something?"

What did the painting tell the police when they came to arrest it?

"I was 'framed'!"

What did the mother piano say to the baby grand?

"I don't like your 'tone,' young man."

What did the quilt say to the bed?

"I've got you 'covered.'"

What did the seven dwarfs' rake say to their hoe?

"Hi, 'hoe.'"

What did the rope say to the phone?

"I can't answer you now. I'm tied up."

What did the mother sewing machine say to her child?

"Because I said 'sew,' that's why."

What did the teddy bear say at the end of the meal?

"I'm 'stuffed.'"

What did the tub say after everyone had taken a bath?

"I'm 'drained.'"

What did one watch say to the other watch?

"Got a minute?"

What did the window say to the doctor?

"I'm in 'pane.'"

What did the window say to the shade?

"You're 'blinding' me."

CARS

What did one amusement-park car say to the other amusement-park car?

"I'm glad I 'bumped' into you."

What did the car say to the bridge?

"You're making me 'cross'!"

What did the car say when it met the road?

"Hi, way.'"

What did the bored race car say to the driver?

"This is a drag."

What did the race car say to the tow truck?

"Now you're 'pulling a fast one.'"

What did one directional signal say to the other directional signal?

"Now it's my turn."

What did the muffler say to the car?

"I'm 'exhausted'!"

What did the tire jack say to the car?

"Can I give you a lift?"

What did one windshield wiper say to the windshield wiper that couldn't make up its mind?

"Quit going back and forth."

CLOTHES

What did the boots say to the firefighter?

"You ride on the truck. I'll go on foot."

What did one side of the seam say to the other side of the seam?

"Let's 'split.'"

What did the panty hose say to the shoes?

"I have to 'run.'"

Why won't the shoes talk to the socks?

They're "tongue-tied."

What did the sock say to the foot?

"You're 'putting me on.'"

FOOD AND DRINKS

What did the bread say when someone left it in the toaster too long?

"This 'burns me up.'"

What did the bread dough say to the baker?

"It's nice to be 'kneaded.'"

What did the bubblegum say to the math book?

"I'm 'stuck' on a problem."

What did the cake batter say to the trouble-making spoon?

"Stop 'stirring things up.'"

What did one cherry in the pie say to the other cherry in the pie?

"Isn't this the 'pits'?"

What did one cornstalk say when the other cornstalk had exciting news?

"I'm all 'ears.'"

What did the egg say to the comedian?

"You 'crack me up.'"

What did one egg say to the other egg?

"Want to hear a 'yolk'?"

What did the scrambled egg say to the piggybank?

"Will you please lend me money? I'm 'broke.'"

What did the hot dog say when it rode the roller coaster?

"Wheeeeeeeeee!-ner."

What did the lemonade say to the ice cube?

"You're 'cool.'"

What did the potato say when the farmer lost his hoe?

"I'll keep my eyes 'peeled' for it."

What did one potato chip say to the other potato chip?

"Let's go for a 'dip.'"

What did one sandwich say when it disagreed with the other sandwich?

"You're full of baloney!"

What did the salad say to the refrigerator?

"Close the door. I'm 'dressing.'"

What did the strawberry say to the jar?

"Help me, please! I'm in a 'jam.'"

What did one sesame seed say to the other sesame seed?

"Don't stop now; we're on a 'roll.'"

What did the sweet potato say when the teacher took attendance?

"Here I 'yam.'"

What did the tired vegetable say?

"I'm 'beet'!"

What did the vegetables say to the stew meat?

"We're all going to 'pot.'"

SPORTS

What did the bowling pins say to the bowling ball?

"Please 'spare' us."

What did the bowling ball say to the bowling pins?

"I can't stop now; I'm on a roll."

What did the football say to the football player?

"Stop kicking me around."

What did one soccer shoe say to the other soccer shoe?

"We're going to have a 'ball.'"

16 Odds and Ends
Riddles about Popular Subjects

BALLET

Why are ballerinas always ready to learn new dance steps?

> They're always "on their toes."

Why did the ballerina wear a tutu?

> The "one-one" was too small and the "three-three" was too big.

Why don't elephants dance ballet?

> They're "tutu" (too, too) big for the costumes.

Where do ballerinas swim?

> "twirl-pools"

How do you make a strawberry swirl?

> Teach it ballet.

See also the Nutcracker riddles under "Christmas" in chapter 13.

CIRCUSES

Why did the circus hire an artist?

> to "draw" crowds

Why did Jack and Jill become circus acrobats?

> They're good at "tumbling."

What does the ringmaster call the tumblers who throw tantrums?

> "acro-brats"

What do bareback riders do when they wait for their turns?

> "hold their horses"

Why did the circus horse think the bareback rider was picking on him?

> She "got on his back."

Why do people who've seen ghosts often become clowns?

> They're "scared silly."

What do clowns get when they stand in front of mirrors?

"funny looks"

What makes contortionists so helpful?

They'll "bend over backward" for you.

What did the circus dog do at the basketball game?

It "jumped through the hoops."

What did the ringmaster call the lion-taming act?

"our 'mane' attraction"

Why doesn't anything ever get past the performing seal?

It's always "on the ball."

How did the performing seal help the circus accountant?

It "balanced" the books.

Why do tightrope walkers carry their checkbooks?

to keep their "balance"

What did the tightrope walker say to the tightrope?

"'Hi, wire.'"

Where do tightrope walkers learn their act?

"high" school

How do trapeze artists feel at the end of their act?

"let down"

Why did the trapeze artist lose her job?

She couldn't "catch on."

EGGS

If an egg came floating down the Mississippi, where did it come from?

a chicken

Where do giant condors come from?

eggs

Where does the chicken always come before the egg?

in dictionaries

What did the chicken grow in its garden?

"egg-plant"

What did the hen name her egg?

Shelly

How did the silly kids try getting egg rolls?

They put their chicken on top of a slide.

How did the silly kids try to get hard-boiled eggs?

They bathed their chickens in hot water.

What did the bullfighter say to his hen?

"'Oh, lay!'"

Why did the hen get booed off the stage during the talent show?

She "laid an egg."

Why do chickens lay eggs?

The eggs would break, if they dropped them.

What lays eggs, clucks, and lives in the ocean?

"chicken of the sea"

Why did the chicken stop in the middle of the road?

to "lay it on the line"

How did the chickens build a wall around their coop?

> by "laying" bricks

What would you get if you crossed the third little pig with a hen?

> a "brick-layer"

What did the chicken bake on her friend's birthday?

> a "layer" cake

Why has the hen stopped laying eggs?

> She's tired of working for chicken feed.

What happens when a chicken stops giving eggs?

> It's "laid off."

What happened when the chicken ate a yo-yo?

> It kept laying the same egg!

What do hens lay when they're sitting on pillows?

> soft-boiled eggs

What do chickens lay during heat waves?

> hard-boiled eggs

What did the hen lay while sitting on top of the slide?

> egg rolls

What do stolen chickens lay?

> "poached" eggs

What do hens lay during earthquakes?

> scrambled eggs

What did the eggs do when they saw a ghost in the kitchen?

> They "scrambled" out of the pan.

What happened when the eggs played football?

> The game turned into a "scramble."

What does Tinker Bell use when she's scrambling eggs?

> a Peter "pan"

How are losing [name any sport] teams like scrambled eggs?

> They're always "beaten."

How are fried eggs like a winning [name any sport] team?

> They can't be "beat."

Why did the eggs scream at the cook?

> He "beat" them.

Why did the silly kid run away from the cookbook?

> It said, "Crack an egg and 'beat it.'"

Where do eggs make friends?

> at "mixers"

How are New Year's resolutions like eggs?

> They're easy to break.

Why does the egg need a loan from the bank?

> It's "broke."

What does the chicken get at the gym?

> "eggs-ercise"

What happened to the chickens that fought in school?

> They got "eggs-pelled."

Why did the chicken buy a skateboard?

> It liked "eggs-treme" sports.

Create new riddles substituting "eggs" for "ex."

How do we know that egg yolks are cowardly?
They're "yellow."

Why didn't the omelet laugh?
It didn't get the "yolk."

Why did the bacon laugh?
The eggs cracked a "yolk."

What happened when the chicken read her eggs riddles?
They "cracked up."

How do clowns enjoy their eggs?
"funny-side" up

What do pilots use for cooking eggs?
"flying" pans

Why don't airline pilots put anything on their eggs?
They like them "plane."

What's the best way to make an egg roll?
Push it down a hill.

See also "Easter" in chapter 13 and "Food and Drinks" in chapter 15.

PIRATES

What does the pirate call his paintings?
"arrrrrrrrt"

What did the pirate get on his report card?
seven "Cs"

What did it cost pirates to get their ears pierced?
a "buccaneer" (buck an ear)

Why did Peg-Leg Pete lose control over his pirate crew?
He couldn't put his foot down.

Why will the pirate save money when he buys a new ship?
There's a "sail" (sale) on it.

What part of a pirate ship is worth twenty-five cents?
the "quarter-deck"

What do pirates order at Godfather's?
"pizzas" (pieces) of eight

Where do pirates go when they join the army?
"booty" camp

What story tells about a pirate cat and its treasure?
"Puss 'n' 'Booty'"

RAIN

What goes up when rain comes down?
umbrellas

What would you get if you crossed a light rain with [name a fictional bear]?
a "drizzly bear"

What do you call it when chickens, turkeys, and ducks fall out of the sky?
"fowl" weather

When does money fall out of the sky?
when there's "change" in the weather

When do gorillas fall out of the sky?
during "Ape-ril" showers

When do booties, rattles, and diapers fall out of the sky?

during baby "showers"

What did the silly kids do when the meteorologist predicted showers?

They took soap outside.

What should you do if it starts raining when you're working on the computer?

Close the "Windows."

What would you get if you crossed a storm cloud with Rudolph?

a "rain-deer"

What should you use to paint pictures of rain?

"water-colors"

Why don't ghosts like to go out in the rain?

It dampens their "spirits."

What's the best way to keep dry when it rains?

Stay inside.

Why do mother kangaroos hate when it rains?

Their kids have to play inside.

What happens when rain beats on your windows?

They have "panes."

Why are veterinarians busiest during thunderstorms?

It "rains cats and dogs."

What's worse than having it rain cats and dogs?

having it "hail" taxis

Where do flowers sleep when it rains?

water "beds"

How do we know that raindrops are clumsy?

They fall a lot.

Why did the raindrop need first aid?

It fell.

What would you get if you crossed a jogger with a raindrop?

"running" water

What do raindrops eat for breakfast?

"Plop-Tarts"

What's the longest stretch of wet weather in the history of England?

Queen Victoria's "reign"

SNOW

When is a boat like a pile of snow?

when it's "adrift" (a drift)

What did the weather forecaster get when he didn't button his coat before going out in a blizzard?

a cold "front"

Why shouldn't you wear snowshoes?

They'll melt when you come inside.

Why can't snowmen remember things?

They're "flaky."

Why was the snowman in trouble?

It "got in hot water."

What do snowmen like to play?

"freeze tag"

What did the police officer say to the snowman who was robbing the bank?

"Freeze!"

What do snowmen eat with spaghetti?

snowballs

What kind of salad do snowmen enjoy?

"cold-slaw"

What did the snowman win at the Olympics?

a "cold" medal

What do snowmen use to pay their bills?

"cold cash"

What did Frosty give the bullies who teased him?

the "cold shoulder"

What would you get if you crossed the snowman that came to life with a shark?

"Frost-bite"

What do you call a snowman on a sunny day?

a puddle

See also reproducible riddles for snowman puppets in appendix C.

SPACE

Aliens

Why do Martians grow beautiful flowers?

They have little green thumbs.

What do aliens eat for breakfast?

flying "sausages"

What do aliens put in cocoa?

"Martian-mallows"

What chickens come from outer space?

"eggs-traterrestrials"

What did the alien say to the library book?

"Take me to your 'reader.'"

What did the alien say to the garden?

"Take me to your 'weeder.'"

What's the best way to see flying saucers?

Trip the waitress.

What would you call a flying saucer filled with sheep from outer space?

a "Ewe-FO"

What would you call a flying saucer filled with cats from outer space?

a "Mew-FO"

How do space cats drink their milk?

from flying "saucers"

Astronauts

What do astronauts take when they're sick?

space "capsules"

What did the astronaut see in the skillet?

unidentified "frying" objects

What do astronauts use for eating?

satellite "dishes"

What kind of tea can't astronauts drink on space missions?

"gravi-tea"

What do you call an astronaut who takes naps near the sun?

a "light" sleeper

What did the astronaut call her poems about outer space?

"uni-verse"

What did Neil Armstrong tie when he was a Boy Scout?

"astro-knots"

See also "Reading" in chapter 7.

Astronomers and Planetariums

Why is the planetarium spectacular?

It's an "all-star show."

What happened when the telescope fell on the astronomer's head?

She saw "stars."

Why are the astronomers happy about their work?

It's "looking up."

Meteors

What keeps astronauts clean in space?

meteor "showers"

Milky Way

Why did the cow jump over the moon?

to get to the Milky Way

Moon

Why do the silly kids think that Africa is farther away than the moon?

They can see the moon.

What holds up the moon?

"moon-beams"

Why couldn't the astronauts get a reservation at the lunar hotel?

The moon was "full."

Which weighs more: a full moon or a crescent moon?

The full moon is "lighter."

How is the moon like a dollar bill?

It has four "quarters."

What part of outer space can you buy for twenty-five cents?

a "quarter" moon

Outer Space

Why can't the students understand the lesson about outer space?

It's over their heads.

What part of our solar system has the most trash?

"Pollute-o" (Pluto)

Why did Mickey Mouse want to go up in space?

to find "Pluto"

Planets

Why did the silly astronaut claim she'd set foot on Mars?

She'd stepped on a candy bar.

What kind of music do astronauts listen to on space missions?

"Nep-tunes"

How can you contact life on Saturn?

Give them a "ring."

What happens when Saturn takes a bath?

It leaves a "ring."

Stars

What's so great about stars?

They're "out of this world."

What would you get if you crossed a boulder with a constellation?

"rock stars"

Why did the silly singer want to go up in space?

to be a "star"

What does the Man on the Moon use to eat soup?

a "Big Dipper"

What constellation makes a mess when it eats soup?

the Big "Dripper"

What constellation do waiters and waitresses look for?

the Big "Tipper"

Create new riddles using words that rhyme with "dipper."

What baseball game is played in outer space?

the "All-Stars" Game

Why do distant stars pass out?

They're "faint."

Sun

What do astronauts use for drinking?

"sun-glasses"

What holds the sun up?

"sun-beams"

What would you get if you crossed a bumble-bee with a sunbeam?

a "sting-ray"

How is a black eye like the sun?

It's a "shiner."

Why does the sun get all As in school?

It's very "bright."

What does the sun keep in its bank account?

daylight "savings"

What happens at the crack of dawn?

Day "breaks."

SUPERHEROES

What happened when Batman and his sidekick went fishing?

Robin ate the worms.

What superhero wears a black cape, has a sidekick named Robin, and throws tantrums all the time?

"Brat-man"

What superhero wears a black cape, has a sidekick named Robin, and gives wool?

"Baaaa-tman"

What does Spider-Man call his really delicious large meatball sandwiches?

"super heroes"

What would you get if you crossed Superman with mollusks?

strong "mussels"

Who can fly, wears an "S" on his chest, and loves eating chicken broth?

    "Soup-erman"

Who can fly, wears an "S" on his chest, and dishes up ice cream faster than a speeding bullet?

    "Scooper-man"

Folktale and Puppet Skits

THE TALKING TURNIP: A FOLKTALE

One long-ago morning, when strange things still happened, a woman was making some soup. One by one, she picked up the vegetables on her table and tossed them into her pot.

When she reached for a turnip, however, it shouted, "Leave me alone! I don't want to be soup."

Startled, the woman looked around to see who had spoken. When she spied her dog lying near the pot, she asked him doubtfully, "Did you say something?"

"No, it was the turnip. It doesn't want you to eat it," explained her cat.

The woman couldn't believe her ears. Usually her cat never even meowed—but now he was talking back to her. And so was a turnip!

As she swung her cooking spoon to swat the cat, a new voice stopped her.

"Don't hurt him!" the pot commanded.

"What?" the old woman gasped and dropped the spoon.

"Ouch!" it yelped when it hit the floor.

"Aaaaaaaaah!" The woman fled her cottage, screaming so loudly she scared the birds right out of the trees. Because people took their troubles to the king in those days, she ran down the road toward the castle.

Whoops! She stumbled over a stone and went sprawling in front of a boy taking geese to the market.

"Are you hurt?" he asked.

The woman leaped to her feet before he could help her up. "No," she replied, panting.

"Why were you running?" asked the boy.

"I need to see the king right away!"

"Why?"

"Things in my cottage were talking to me! While I was making soup, a turnip asked me to leave it alone. Then my cat said, 'It doesn't want you to eat it.' When I tried to swat my cat for talking back, the pot said, 'Don't hurt him.' That scared me so badly, I dropped my spoon and it yelled, 'Ouch!' I need to ask the king what I should do."

"He probably won't believe you," the boy told her. "Why not go home and save yourself the long walk to the castle?"

"Throw the turnip in the pot when you get there," said the goose under his left arm.

"Don't let it boss you around," added the goose under his right arm.

"Aaaaaaaaah!" screamed the boy, flinging his arms in the air. While the geese flapped to freedom, the boy and the woman sped toward the castle as if their heels were the ones that had wings.

Not far from the castle, the woman bumped into a woodcutter, jostling the ax he carried over his shoulder.

"Watch where you're going," the woodcutter warned. "Why are you hurrying, anyway?"

"We have to see the king right away!"

"Why?"

"Strange things keep happening! First a turnip asked me to leave it alone. Then my cat said, 'It doesn't want you to eat it.' I tried to swat my cat for talking back, but the pot said, 'Don't hurt him.' When I dropped my spoon, it yelled, 'Ouch!'"

Then the boy blurted, "When I told her to go home, one of my geese said, 'Throw the turnip in the pot when you get there,' and the other said, 'Don't let it boss you around.'"

"Is that all?" the woodcutter asked scornfully. "Is that why you're running?"

"You'd run, too, if that happened to you," said his ax.

"Aaaaaaaaah!" screamed the woodcutter, hurling his ax as far as he could. All three raced to the castle and banged on its door.

A guard opened it. "Shh! The king is meeting with his advisors."

"But we need to see him right away! It's important!" cried the woman.

"You can't disturb him now. You'll have to wait." The guard wouldn't let them into the throne room until the king's advisors had left.

Weary and out of sorts from arguing with his advisors, the king was dismayed to see three more people he'd have to deal with. "What brings you here? Why aren't you out working?" he demanded.

"I *was* working, Your Majesty! That's when the trouble began!" cried the woman.

"What trouble?" asked the king.

"Everything started talking to me! First a turnip asked me to leave it alone. Then my cat said, 'It doesn't want you to eat it.' When I tried to swat my cat for talking back, the pot said, 'Don't hurt him.' I got so scared, I dropped the spoon, and it yelled, 'Ouch!'"

The boy spoke next. "My geese talked, too! One said, 'Throw the turnip in the pot when you get there,' and the other said, 'Don't let it boss you around.'"

"That's not all!" added the woodcutter. "My ax said, 'You'd run, too, if that happened to you.'"

The king thundered, "How *dare* you bother me with ridiculous lies? Go back to work before I punish you for wasting valuable time."

Heads hanging, the woman, the boy, and the woodcutter slunk out of the castle.

"You *should* have punished them, Your Majesty," said the guard. "People spouting nonsense like that are nothing but troublemakers."

"Nonsense indeed! Whoever heard of a turnip that talks?" scoffed the king's crown.

The End

THE GHOST BRIDGE: A HALLOWEEN PUPPET SKIT

CHARACTERS: Child (boy or girl; right hand); Ghost (left hand)
PROPS: pencil, sheet of paper

SCENE 1: A Day in October

PUPPETEER: It is a day in October. Pretend there's a bridge on my left side.
CHILD: (runs in stage right and crosses stage)
GHOST: (pops out from behind your back, stage left, shouting) Boo!
CHILD: (gasps and jumps back) You scared me!
GHOST: That's what ghosts do. What do *you* do?
CHILD: I go to school.
GHOST: Why?
CHILD: My mother makes me.
GHOST: Why?
CHILD: She *says* she wants me to learn stuff so I'll be smart, but *I* think she just wants to get me out of the house all day.
GHOST: You're probably right about that.
CHILD: Will you please move out of my way? I have to cross the bridge because my new school's on the other side. Today's my first day and I don't want to be late.
GHOST: *No* one can cross this bridge.

CHILD: Why not?

GHOST: (mysteriously) Haven't you heard the story of the ghost bridge?

CHILD: (shakes head) No.

GHOST: That's funny. I thought it was a staple at campfires and sleepovers for miles around.

CHILD: My mom and I just moved here. Back home we told stories about the Headless Horseman and the haunted hitchhiker.

GHOST: Pooh! The story of the ghost bridge is *much* scarier.

CHILD: Why? What happens?

GHOST: (ominously) On a dark and stormy night, when the wind howled like a banshee [howl] and the rain poured down in buckets, a little girl and her mother were crossing this bridge. The girl slipped on a puddle and tumbled headfirst into the raging waters. Immediately, her mother plunged in to save her, but it was hopeless. The black, inky depths swallowed them up. Their bodies were never recovered.

CHILD: (gasps) How dreadful!

GHOST: Ever since, their ghosts have haunted the bridge and refused to let anyone cross. On dark and stormy nights, you can still hear the little girl's terrified cry, "Mommy, helllllllllllllp!" and her mother's anguished wail, "My baby! Oh, my baaaaaaaaaaa-beeeeeeeeee!"

CHILD: And I thought starting a new school in the middle of the semester was scary.

GHOST: You won't be starting a new school, because I am the ghost of the girl who drowned. If you try to cross the bridge, I'll haunt you. (flies around Child, moaning and wailing)

CHILD: If I don't cross this bridge and go to school, my mom will take away my cell phone. Then I can't call my friends back home.

GHOST: Get out your stationery, kid. You'll have to write letters to keep in touch.

CHILD: (screams) Now *that's* scary! (thinks a minute) Can we make a deal?

GHOST: What kind of deal?

CHILD: I'll ask you a riddle. If you can answer it, I won't cross your bridge. If you can't, I get to cross without your haunting me.

GHOST: What's the riddle?

CHILD: Why does an elephant have a trunk?

GHOST: (puts hand to head and tips head slightly, as if thinking very hard) Hmmmmmmmmm. (straightens up and looks right at Child) What's an elephant?

CHILD: A big animal with a trunk.

GHOST: Oh. (thinks) Hmmmmmmmmm.

CHILD: Give up?

GHOST: (crossly) Yes!

CHILD: It doesn't have a glove compartment. (jumps up and down) I win! I win! I get to cross the bridge! (exits stage left)

GHOST: (wails and disappears behind your back)

SCENE 2: The Next Day

PUPPETEER: Now it's the next day.

CHILD: (enters stage right and crosses stage) I hope that ghost isn't here today.

GHOST: (pops out from behind your back, at stage left) Boo!

CHILD: (gasps and jumps back)

GHOST: What are you doing here?

CHILD: I have to cross the bridge again.

GHOST: Why?

CHILD: I need to go to school.

GHOST: Why? You went yesterday.

CHILD: You don't learn everything you need to know in just one day.

GHOST: Didn't you learn enough to get by?

CHILD: My mother doesn't think so.

GHOST: Speaking of mothers, mine heard us talking yesterday. She said I shouldn't let you ask me riddles, because you're trying to fool me.

CHILD: Then why don't you ask me a riddle instead?

GHOST: OK.

CHILD: (looks directly at Ghost)

GHOST: (looks back at Child)

CHILD: (moves closer to Ghost and looks directly at her)

GHOST: (looks back at Child)

CHILD: (moves closer to Ghost and looks directly at her)

GHOST: (looks back at Child)

CHILD: (moves right up to Ghost and puts face almost in hers)

GHOST: What? What? Why are you staring at me?

CHILD: I'm not staring. I'm just waiting for you to ask me a riddle.

GHOST: Oh, yeah. I have to ask you a riddle.

CHILD: (expectantly) Well?

GHOST: (irritably) Well, what?

CHILD: What's the riddle?

GHOST: Oh, yeah . . . the riddle. (thinks first and then shakes head) I don't know any.

CHILD: I know a really, really hard one. (whispers in Ghost's ear)

GHOST: (laughs) That one's so hard, you might as well give up right now. You could guess for a million, billion, trillion years and never get the answer.

CHILD: Why don't you ask me anyway?

GHOST: OK. But you'll be sorry because this is really, *really* hard. How many jellybeans can you put in an empty jar that's nine and three-fourths inches high and three and one-sixteenth inches deep?

CHILD: Ooh, math. That *is* hard. (thinks)

GHOST: (laughs) I told you you'll never get it. Do you give up?

CHILD: I guess so . . . No, wait! I just remembered: the size of the jar doesn't matter. You can put only one jellybean into an empty jar, because after that it isn't empty. I win! I win! I get to cross the bridge! (exits stage left)

GHOST: (wails and disappears behind your back)

SCENE 3: The Third Day

PUPPETEER: Now it's the third day.

CHILD: (enters stage right, carrying pencil and piece of paper, and crosses stage) I hope that ghost isn't here today, but I'm ready if she is.

GHOST: (pops out from behind your back, stage left) Boo!

CHILD: (gasps and jumps back)

GHOST: Why did you come back?

CHILD: My mother's still making me go to school to learn stuff.

GHOST: And *my* mother and I still don't want you to cross our bridge.

CHILD: Would you like to ask me another riddle?

GHOST: No! Your riddles make my mother mad. She heard us yesterday, and she said you fooled me again because you knew the answer to that riddle before you told it to me.

CHILD: OK, no riddles, but how about this? Name a color, any color. If I can write that color with my pencil, I get to cross the river.

GHOST: And if you can't, you'll go away forever?

CHILD: Yes.

GHOST: Can I pick *any* color?

CHILD: Yes.

GHOST: Even a weird color, like fuchsia or puce?

CHILD: Yes.

GHOST: (suspiciously) Is that some kind of special trick pencil?

CHILD: No. See for yourself. (holds pencil out toward Ghost)

GHOST: (looks at both sides of the pencil very closely and carefully) It looks like an ordinary pencil.

CHILD: Then do we have a deal? You name a color and I'll write it with this plain, ordinary pencil.

GHOST: You mean you'll *try.*

CHILD: Right. What color do you want me to write?

GHOST: (thinks) Magenta!

CHILD: (writes each letter in the color's name on paper) M-a-g-e-n-t-a!
(holds up paper) See? I win! I win! I get to cross the bridge.
(exits stage left)
GHOST: (wails and disappears behind your back)

SCENE 4: The Fourth Day

PUPPETEER: Now it's the fourth day.
CHILD: (enters stage right and crosses stage) I hope that ghost has given up.
GHOST: (pops out from behind your back, stage left) Boo!
CHILD: (gasps and jumps back)
GHOST: You came back again, eh?
CHILD: Yes. My mother still says I have to go to school and learn stuff.
GHOST: You know what *my* mother says?
CHILD: (fearfully) What?
GHOST: She says that your mother is right. School *does* make you smart,
so she's making me go learn stuff, too. (puts arm around Child)
Come on, kid, let's go. (they both exit stage left)

THE RIDDLE BOOK: A PUPPET SKIT

CHARACTERS: Miggs (left hand); Jiggs (right hand)
PROPS: riddle book you've made
HOW TO PREPARE: To make a riddle book, photocopy this script.
Punch three holes along the left-hand side and put it into a folder that
fastens with clasps or a three-ring binder. Write "Big Book of Riddles" on
the cover. Add tabs to the script to make turning pages easier. (Or trim
their margins and glue pages onto dividers before putting them into the
folder or binder.)

Lay the riddle book in your lap or on a stage. Make Miggs appear to be
reading.

MIGGS: (reads and laughs)
JIGGS: (enters stage right) What's so funny?
MIGGS: I'm reading riddles. See? (holds up book)
JIGGS: Read some to me. I like to laugh.
MIGGS: OK. (reads) Pretend you're dreaming that your house is on fire.
JIGGS: That's not a dream; that's a nightmare!
MIGGS: Don't interrupt. You have only enough time to save either your
mother *or* your father. What should you do?
JIGGS: Ooh, that's hard. I'd want to save both.
MIGGS: According to this riddle, though, you can save only one. What
will you do?

JIGGS: I don't know. What do you think I should do?

MIGGS: Wake up. It was only a dream. (laughs)

JIGGS: Thank heavens. Ask me another riddle, but don't make it so scary.

MIGGS: OK. (reads) When can you carry water in your bare hands?

JIGGS: All the time.

MIGGS: You cannot!

JIGGS: Sure, I can. I carry a water bottle around in my bare hands all the time.

MIGGS: I'm not talking about water in a bottle. I'm talking about water that's not in any kind of container.

JIGGS: Oh. I can't do that. I tried once, but the water kept slipping through my fingers. That's why I bought a water bottle.

MIGGS: You *can* carry water in your bare hands—*if* you freeze it first.

JIGGS: I wouldn't want to do that. Carrying ice would make my hands cold.

MIGGS: Don't be so literal. (reads) What can you break without even touching it?

JIGGS: My mother's vase.

MIGGS: That's not the answer.

JIGGS: But I *did* break my mother's vase without touching it. I was wearing my backpack and that brushed against the vase and knocked it off the table.

MIGGS: That may be, but the answer to the riddle is "a promise."

JIGGS: Huh?

MIGGS: When you don't do what you say you'll do, you break your promise.

JIGGS: Oh, yeah. Now it's my turn to ask you a riddle.

MIGGS: OK.

JIGGS: What's purple, hangs from the ceiling, and whistles?

MIGGS: I have no idea.

JIGGS: (shouts) A catfish!

MIGGS: That doesn't make any sense. A catfish isn't purple.

JIGGS: It is if you paint it.

MIGGS: A catfish doesn't hang from the ceiling.

JIGGS: It does if you put it there.

MIGGS: A catfish doesn't whistle.

JIGGS: I know. I just threw that in to make the riddle harder to guess.

MIGGS: You made that up, didn't you?

JIGGS: (sounds surprised) How did you know? Now I'm going home to see if my parents can figure it out.

MIGGS: They'll never guess. Why don't you ask this one instead? (reads) Who is my father's son and my mother's son but isn't my brother?

JIGGS: Of course, it can't be your brother. You don't have any.

MIGGS: I know.

JIGGS: And it can't be your sister either, because you don't have any.

MIGGS: That's right.

JIGGS: But you have lots of cousins. Is it one of them?

MIGGS: Nope.

JIGGS: Your uncle?

MIGGS: No.

JIGGS: Your grandpa?

MIGGS: No!

JIGGS: Your great-grandpa?

MIGGS: Stop. You're just guessing.

JIGGS: (sounds surprised) How did you know?

MIGGS: The answer is "I."

JIGGS: You?

MIGGS: Yes, "I."

JIGGS: Before I ask my parents, let me see if I have it right. Who is my father's son and my mother's son but isn't my brother?

MIGGS: That's the question. Do you remember the answer?

JIGGS: Yes. You.

MIGGS: No!

JIGGS: But you said you were the answer!

MIGGS: That was when *I* was asking the riddle. If *you're* asking it, the answer is you.

JIGGS: That's what I said: "You."

MIGGS: You're not supposed to say "you," because you're the answer when you're asking.

JIGGS: If you're the answer, why can't I say "you"?

MIGGS: Because when you say "you," you mean me, and the answer when you're asking is you.

JIGGS: I *said* "you."

MIGGS: You're not supposed to say "you."

JIGGS: But you said "you're the answer." I'm confused.

MIGGS: You certainly are. Why don't you go to the library and borrow a riddle book to read to your parents? You can't mess that up too much.

JIGGS: I'll go right now. I love visiting the library. 'Bye. (exits stage right)

MIGGS: (addresses audience) I know a riddle no one will ever be able to answer: How does Jiggs manage to get so confused? I think I'll go to the library, too, and get another riddle book. Hope you'll visit it soon. 'Bye. (exits stage right)

THE PUNCH LINE: A PUPPET SKIT

CHARACTERS: Miggs (left hand); Jiggs (right hand)
PROPS: none

MIGGS: Hi, Jiggs. Would you like some riddles?
JIGGS: No, thanks. I just ate lunch.
MIGGS: (sounds confused) What does eating lunch have to do with riddles?
JIGGS: I'm so full, I couldn't eat another bite.
MIGGS: You don't eat riddles.
JIGGS: Then what do you do with them?
MIGGS: You use them to make people laugh.
JIGGS: Oh, you tickle people with them.
MIGGS: No!
JIGGS: But tickling makes people laugh. (tickles Miggs)
MIGGS: (drops down on stage or in your lap and rolls around, laughing) Stop, stop.
JIGGS: (stops)
MIGGS: (stands up) You don't tickle people with riddles. Riddles are questions you ask.
JIGGS: I'm good at asking questions. Why is the sky blue? Why does the moon change shape? What makes it snow? (sounds really puzzled) Why aren't you laughing?
MIGGS: Because those questions aren't riddles. Their answers are facts. Riddles are pretend questions that have funny answers.
JIGGS: I don't get it.
MIGGS: Let me ask you a riddle, and you'll see what I mean. What would you get if you poured boiling water down a rabbit hole?
JIGGS: (angrily) I'd never do that! That's mean!
MIGGS: I know.
JIGGS: Then why are you talking about it?
MIGGS: It's just for fun.
JIGGS: It's not fun for the rabbits.
MIGGS: I promise that no rabbits will get hurt. Now please say, "I don't know, Miggs, what *would* you get if you poured boiling water down a rabbit hole?"
JIGGS: I don't want to know. I still think it's a mean thing to do.
MIGGS: Come on, Jiggs. Please ask.
JIGGS: (sighs heavily) OK, but only because it means so much to you. "What would you get if you poured boiling water down a rabbit hole?"
MIGGS: "Hot, cross bunnies."
JIGGS: The bunnies wouldn't be the only cross ones. I imagine the SPCA would be angry, too.

MIGGS: Jiggs, you missed the point. I'm not really going to pour hot water down a rabbit hole. I just said that to set up the punch line.

JIGGS: You're serving punch? I don't see anyone lining up for punch. (looks around) I don't see any punch either.

MIGGS: A punch line isn't a row of people waiting for a drink. A punch line is a funny answer to a riddle.

JIGGS: What's funny about poor, scalded bunnies?

MIGGS: There aren't really any poor, scalded bunnies. "Hot, cross bunnies" is just a play on "hot-cross buns."

JIGGS: Oh, you're serving buns with the punch? But I already told you, I'm not hungry.

MIGGS: Jiggs, let's forget about the rabbit joke.

JIGGS: Good. It wasn't funny.

MIGGS: Here's another riddle. Why do bears sleep all winter?

JIGGS: They wouldn't be able to find enough food in the snow.

MIGGS: That's not the right answer.

JIGGS: Yes, it is. My teacher told me that.

MIGGS: I'm sure she did. But that's not the answer to the riddle.

JIGGS: (heatedly) Are you calling my teacher a liar?

MIGGS: No.

JIGGS: Good, because my teacher would never lie. If she says bears sleep all winter because there's no food for them to eat, then that's why they sleep.

MIGGS: Of course, that's why bears *really* sleep all winter. But this is a riddle. I'm not looking for a real, logical reason. I'm looking for a silly answer.

JIGGS: That's silly. Why would you look for pretend answers when you know the real ones?

MIGGS: It's just so we can laugh. Please say, "I don't know, Miggs, why do bears sleep all winter?"

JIGGS: (sighs heavily) OK, if it will make you happy. "Why do bears sleep all winter?"

MIGGS: Their alarm clocks are broken.

JIGGS: I don't think bears have alarm clocks.

MIGGS: Of course, they don't.

JIGGS: Then why did you say they did?

MIGGS: Because it's a funny way to answer the riddle.

JIGGS: You don't know much about animals, do you? You should go to the library and read books about them.

MIGGS: Let's try one more riddle, Jiggs. This one won't be about animals.

JIGGS: Good.

MIGGS: A penny and a quarter sat on a bridge. The penny jumped off. Why didn't the quarter?

JIGGS: It didn't have legs.

MIGGS: That's not the answer.

JIGGS: But quarters *don't* have legs.

MIGGS: Well, pennies don't have legs either.

JIGGS: That's right. So the penny couldn't have jumped off the bridge.

MIGGS: Of course, a penny can't *really* jump off a bridge. But this is supposed to be a joke. *Pretend* a penny could jump off a bridge.

JIGGS: You mean, the way I'm supposed to pretend that bears have alarm clocks?

MIGGS: That's right.

JIGGS: You have a strange imagination.

MIGGS: It's just for fun, Jiggs. Now, the reason that the quarter didn't jump off the bridge when the penny did is because the quarter has a lot more "cents."

JIGGS: Huh?

MIGGS: Don't you get it? The quarter is worth twenty-five cents. The penny is worth only one cent. So the quarter has a lot more cents than the penny, right?

JIGGS: If you say so. I'm not very good with money and math.

MIGGS: You're not very good with wordplay either. The word c-e-n-t-s sounds a lot like s-e-n-s-e. It doesn't make s-e-n-s-e sense to jump off a bridge. That's why the quarter didn't jump.

JIGGS: I still don't think a quarter or a penny could jump. They could roll off if someone happened to kick them though. Is that what happened?

MIGGS: (sounds exasperated) I give up. I'm not going to ask you any more riddles. You just don't understand how to play with words for fun.

JIGGS: (indignantly) I do *so* know how to play with words! I'd take them to the park.

MIGGS: (laughs) That's a good one, Jiggs! That's really funny!

JIGGS: (sounds doubtful) It is?

MIGGS: Sure, you just made a play on the word "play." You made up your own riddle.

JIGGS: I did?

MIGGS: Sure, you did. What's the best way for writers to play with words? Take them to the park. Well, excuse me, Jiggs. I have to go write that down before I forget. (exits stage left, laughing)

JIGGS: (looks out at the audience and shakes his head) I don't know why Miggs was laughing so hard. Playing in the park really *is* fun. Oh, well. All this talking's made me thirsty. I'm going to look for that punch line Miggs talked about. 'Bye. (exits stage right)

Recommended Riddle Books

What happened when the lion read a riddle book?

It "roared" with laughter.

Not every riddle in these books will make readers roar with laughter, but of the many collections I read that are still in print, I liked the following titles best. Except for Katy Hall and Lisa Eisenberg's riddle books for Dial, I don't recommend buying whole series. Titles vary in quality, and some contain more jokes than riddles. These books were all available through Bound to Stay Bound, Follett, or Perma-Bound in November 2006. Titles marked with an asterisk (*) index riddles by topic; titles marked with a dagger (†) group riddles into chapters by subject matter.

STORIES WITH RIDDLES

Mooser, Stephen. *Smell That Clue!* Grosset and Dunlap, 2006. (easy chapter book)
   A young detective tries to answer a riddle *and* find an important paper.

Pfeffer, Susan Beth. *The Riddle Streak*. Henry Holt, 1993. (easy chapter book)
   Amy wants to beat her big brother at something. When she can't find a riddle he doesn't already know, she makes some up.

Thaler, Mike. *The Substitute Teacher from the Black Lagoon*. Scholastic, 2005. (picture book)
   The fearsome-looking substitute teacher doesn't seem so scary when he lets the class make a state riddle book during geography. Consider making your own riddle books after reading this. (See "Mini Ha-Ha's" in chapter 2.)

Wolff, Patricia Rae. *The Toll-Bridge Troll.* Harcourt, Brace, 2000. (picture book)
A boy uses riddles to outwit a troll.

FOR BEGINNING READERS

Each book has either one or two color illustrations per simple riddle.

Brown, Marc Tolon. *Spooky Riddles.* Beginner Books, 1983.
Cerf, Bennett. *Riddles and More Riddles!* Random House, 1999.
Dahl, Michael. *Alphabet Soup: A Book of Riddles about Letters.* Picture Window Books, 2004.
———. *Animal Quack-Ups: Foolish and Funny Jokes about Animals.* Picture Window Books, 2003.
———. *Chewy Chuckles: Deliciously Funny Jokes about Food.* Picture Window Books, 2003.
———. *Galactic Giggles: Far-Out and Funny Jokes about Outer Space.* Picture Window Books, 2003.
———. *Laughs on a Leash: A Book of Pet Jokes.* Picture Window Books, 2004.
———. *Monster Laughs: Frightfully Funny Jokes about Monsters.* Picture Window Books, 2003.
———. *School Buzz: Classy and Funny Jokes about School.* Picture Window Books, 2003.
———. *Three-Alarm Jokes: A Book of Firefighter Jokes.* Picture Window Books, 2004.
———. *Under Arrest: A Book of Police Jokes.* Picture Window Books, 2004.
———. *Zoodles: A Book of Riddles about Animals.* Picture Window Books, 2004.
Hall, Katy, and Lisa Eisenberg. *Stinky Riddles.* Dial, 2005. (Their other riddle books for Dial and Puffin are OK, too.)

FOR GRADES 2–4

Each page has several riddles. Many pages have a small color picture to illustrate one of their riddles.

Cole, Joanna. *Why Did the Chicken Cross the Road? And Other Riddles, Old and New.* Morrow Junior Books, 1994. (Unlike the others, this has line drawings.)
Dahl, Michael. *Roaring with Laugher: A Book of Animal Jokes.* Picture Window Books, 2005.
———. *Sit! Stay! Laugh! A Book of Pet Jokes.* Picture Window Books, 2005.

Donahue, Jill L. *Artful Antics: A Book of Art, Music, and Theater Jokes.* Picture Window Books, 2007.

———. *How Do You Get There? A Book of Transportation Jokes.* Picture Window Books, 2007.

———. *Silly Sports: A Book of Sports Jokes.* Picture Window Books, 2007.

———. *What's in a Name? A Book of Name Jokes.* Picture Window Books, 2007.

Horsfall, Jacqueline. *Funny Riddles.* Sterling, 2006.*

Moore, Mark. *Beastly Laughs: A Book of Monster Jokes.* Picture Window Books, 2005.

———. *Creepy Crawlers: A Book of Bug Jokes.* Picture Window Books, 2004.

———. *Spooky Sillies: A Book of Ghost Jokes.* Picture Window Books, 2004.

Peterson, Scott K., et al. *Let the Fun Begin: Wacky What-Do-You-Get Jokes, Playful Puns, and More.* Carolrhoda, 2005.

Rissinger, Matt and Philip Yates. *Wacky Jokes.* Sterling, 2003.*

Rosenberg, Pam. *Animal Jokes.* Child's World, 2005.

———. *Historical Jokes.* Child's World, 2005.

———. *Holiday Jokes.* Child's World, 2004.

———. *Riddles.* Child's World, 2004.

———. *School Jokes.* Child's World, 2005.

Rosenbloom, Joseph. *School Jokes.* Sterling, 2003.*

———. *Spooky Jokes.* Sterling, 2005.*

Schultz, Sam. *Game-Day Gigglers: Winning Jokes to Score Some Laughs.* Carolrhoda, 2004.

Swanson, June. *Punny Places: Jokes to Make You Mappy.* Carolrhoda, 2004.

Walton, Rick, and Ann Walton. *Magical Mischief: Jokes That Shock and Amaze.* Carolrhoda, 2005.

———. *The Sky's the Limit: Naturally Funny Jokes.* Carolrhoda, 2005.

Ziegler, Mark. *Chitchat Chuckles: A Book of Funny Talk.* Picture Window Books, 2006.

———. *Critter Jitters: A Book of Animal Jokes.* Picture Window Books, 2004.

———. *Giggle Bubbles: A Book of Underwater Jokes.* Picture Window Books, 2005.

———. *Goofballs: A Book of Sports Jokes.* Picture Window Books, 2005.

———. *Lunchbox Laughs: A Book of Food Jokes.* Picture Window Books, 2005.

———. *Nutty Names: A Book of Name Jokes.* Picture Window Books, 2006.

———. *School Kidders: A Book of School Jokes.* Picture Window Books, 2005.

———. *Wacky Wheelies: A Book of Transportation Jokes.* Picture Window Books, 2005.

FOR GRADES 4 AND UP

Every page contains many riddles. Most books have only a few line drawings.

Fox, Lori Miller. *Riddle Riot.* Sterling, 2003.*†
Grambs, Alison. *Totally Silly Jokes.* Sterling, 2003.*†
Horsfall, Jacqueline. *Joke and Riddle Ballyhoo.* Sterling, 2005.*†
———. *Super Goofy Jokes.* Sterling, 2004.*†
Rosenbloom, Joseph. *Biggest Riddle Book in the World.* Sterling, 1976.*† (If you could buy only one book, I'd recommend this. It has a wealth of riddles for all ages. A few are outdated.)
Thomas, Lyn. *Ha! Ha! Ha! 1,000+ Jokes, Riddles, Facts, and More.* Owl Books, 2001.*†

BOOKS REFERRED TO IN THE TEXT

Anderson, Dee. *Amazingly Easy Puppet Plays.* ALA Editions, 1997.
Bernstein, Joanne E. *Fiddle with a Riddle: Write Your Own Riddles.* Dutton, 1979.
Burns Marilyn. *The Hink Pink Book; or, What Do You Call a Magician's Extra Bunny?* Little, Brown, 1981.
Cerf, Bennett. *Riddle-De-Dee.* 1964; repr., Random House, 1994.
Chocolate, Deborah M. Newton. *Talk, Talk: An Ashanti Legend.* Troll Associates, 1993.
Hepworth, Cathi. *ANTics! An Alphabetical Anthology.* Putnam, 1992.
McCall, Francis X. *A Huge Hog Is a Big Pig: A Rhyming Word Game.* Greenwillow, 2002.
Most, Bernard. *There's an Ant in Anthony.* HarperTrophy, 1992.
Rasinski, Timothy V. *The Fluent Reader.* Scholastic Professional Books, 2003.
Terban, Marvin. *Eight Ate: A Feast of Homonym Riddles.* Clarion, 2007.
———. *Funny You Should Ask: How to Make Up Jokes and Riddles with Wordplay.* Clarion, 1992.
Thaler, Mike. *Funny Side Up! How to Create Your Own Riddles.* Scholastic, 1985.
Wolff, Patricia Rae. *The Toll-Bridge Troll.* Harcourt, Brace, 2000.

BUYING RIDDLE BOOKS TO GIVE AWAY
OR SUPPLEMENT YOUR COLLECTION

School book fairs carry riddle books, some for only ninety-nine cents. School book clubs sometimes offer riddle books. Check teacher offers as well as student order forms. Quality varies, but you can stock up on the cheapest ones to give away in drawings or fill a heavy demand.

Shop thrift shops, yard sales, and library sales for riddle books in good condition. Look for old copies of *Highlights* and *Ranger Rick*, too, because every issue has riddles.

APPENDIX

Reproducibles and Samples

Also visit the book's website for downloadable versions of these reproducibles: www.ala.org/editions/extras/Anderson09577.

From Dee Anderson, *Reading Is Funny!* (Chicago: ALA, 2009).

What did the
mother broom
say to her
little broom?

"I've always
'looked up'
to you."

How did the
needle say
good-bye to the
thread?

"Good night,
'sweep' tight.
Don't let the
bedbugs bite."

What did the
pencil sharpener
say to the pencil?

"'Sew' long."

What did the
kitchen floor say to
the ceiling?

"Let's get
to the 'point.'"

What did the
scissors say
to the hair?

"It won't be long now."

What did one wall say to the other wall?

"Let's 'catch some rays.'"

What did the vacuum cleaner say to the maid?

"I'll meet you at the corner."

What did the tie say to the hat?

"I don't like when you push me around!"

What did one baseball glove say to the other glove on a sunny day?

"You go on 'a head.' I'll 'hang around' here."

What did the
football say
to the football
player?

"You go ahead.
I'll 'ketchup'
(catch up)."

YOU WIN!

"Stop kicking
me around!"

How did
the ocean
say hello to
the beach?

What did the
bubblegum say
when it flunked
the test?

What did
one tomato
say to the
other tomato?

It "waved."

"I 'blew it'!"

From Dee Anderson, *Reading Is Funny!* (Chicago: ALA, 2009).

America's
National Bird
598.942

by
Moe Grass

How Chocolate
Is Made
641.3374

by
E. Gull

The Little
Tattletale
E

by
Candy Barr

Make Money
This Summer
650.12

by
I. Will Tell

Weeds
in Your Backyard
583

by Dan D. Lyons	*Animals on the Farm* 636	by April Showers
Animals in Winter 591.56	by Nan E. Goat	*Your Pet Dog* 636.7
by Hi Burr Nation	*One Rainy Spring Day* E	by Kay Nine

From Dee Anderson, *Reading Is Funny!* (Chicago: ALA, 2009).

CAN YOU NAME THE AUTHOR?

*A Day at
the Beach*
E

by
Lotta Snow

Spring Gardening
635

by
C. Shores

*Working for the
Post Office*
383.145

by
Mae Flowers

*All About
Blizzards*
551.55

by
May L. Carrier

YOU WIN!

CAN YOU FILL IN THE BLANKS?

Match each animal to its riddle.

1. What do _____ do when they get into trouble?
    "weasel" their way out

2. Why did the _____ get in trouble at the library?
    It chased the computer mouse.

3. What did Christopher Robin name his pet _____?
    Winnie-the-"Pew"

4. What would you get if you crossed a centipede with a _____?
    a walkie-talkie

5. What did the baseball slugger buy for his pet _____?
    a batting cage

6. Why did the _____ get splinters in its tongue?
    It ate table scraps.

7. How can you learn how to care for your pet _____?
    Search the "Fin-ternet."

8. How can you keep your pet _____ from squeaking?
    Oil them.

a.	parrot	d.	cat	g.	ferrets
b.	mice	e.	dog	h.	canary
c.	fish	f.	skunk		

From Dee Anderson, *Reading Is Funny!* (Chicago: ALA, 2009).

WHO SAID THAT?

Match each question on the left side to its answer on the right side.

1. What did the mother broom say to her little broom?

    a. "I don't like when you push me around!"

2. What did the kitchen floor say to the ceiling?

    b. "You go on 'a head.' I'll 'hang around' here."

3. What did the pencil sharpener say to the pencil?

    c. "'Sew' long."

4. How did the needle say good-bye to the thread?

    d. It "waved."

5. What did the scissors say to the hair?

    e. "I'll meet you at the corner."

6. How did the ocean say hello to the beach?

    f. "Good night, 'sweep' tight. Don't let the bedbugs bite."

7. What did one wall say to the other wall?

    g. "Let's 'catch some rays.'"

8. What did one baseball glove say to the other glove on a sunny day?

    h. "I've always 'looked up' to you."

9. What did the tie say to the hat?

    i. "Let's get to the 'point.'"

10. What did the vacuum cleaner say to the maid?

    j. "It won't be long now."

WHO WROTE THAT?

Match each pretend book on the left side with its
imaginary author on the right side.

1. Who wrote *America's National Bird*? (598.942)   a.   Nan E. Goat

2. Who wrote *Make Money This Summer*? (650.12)   b.   Hi Burr Nation

3. Who wrote *Your Pet Dog*? (636.7)   c.   C. Shores

4. Who wrote *Animals on the Farm*? (636)   d.   Moe Grass

5. Who wrote *All about Blizzards*? (551.55)   e.   Dan D. Lyons

6. Who wrote *A Day at the Beach*? (E)   f.   I. Will Tell

7. Who wrote *How Chocolate Is Made*? (641.3374)   g.   Kay Nine

8. Who wrote *Animals in Winter*? (591.56)   h.   Lotta Snow

9. Who wrote *Weeds in Your Backyard*? (583)   i.   Candy Barr

10. Who wrote *The Little Tattletale*? (E)   j.   E. Gull

   From Dee Anderson, *Reading Is Funny!* (Chicago: ALA, 2009).

CRACK THE CODE!

Can You Figure Out the Secret Answers?

Write the letter that comes *after* each letter in the answers. For example, the first answer starts with "f" because "f" comes after "e" in the alphabet. Write "a" after every "z."

1. What do clowns get when they stand in front of mirrors?   "etmmx knnjr"

   "_ _ _ _ _   _ _ _ _ _"

2. What would you get if you crossed an athlete with an automobile?   z "ronqsr" bzq

   _ _   "_ _ _ _ _ _"   _ _ _

3. What would you call a panda without any teeth?   z "ftllx" adzq

   _ _   "_ _ _ _ _"   _ _ _ _

4. Who can fly, wears an "S" on his chest, and dishes up ice cream faster than a speeding bullet?   "Rbnnodq-lzm"

   "_ _ _ _ _ _ _ _ – _ _ _"

5. What was the spider doing in the outfield?   bzsbghmf "ekhdr"

   _ _ _ _ _ _ _ _ _   "_ _ _ _ _"

6. Why did the hair call the beautician a bully?   Rgd "sdzrdc" hs.

   _ _ _   "_ _ _ _ _ _"   _ _.

7. What invention lets people walk through walls?   cnnqr

   _ _ _ _ _

A B C D E F G H I J K L M N O P Q R S T U V W X Y Z

From Dee Anderson, *Reading Is Funny!* (Chicago: ALA, 2009).

Sample handout for back of Crack the Code! activity sheet

LAUGH IT UP WITH RIDDLE BOOKS

 from
[your library's
name]

For Beginning Readers

Brown, Marc. *Spooky Riddles*
Cerf, Bennett. *Riddles and More Riddles!*
Dahl, Michael. *Alphabet Soup*
_____. *Animal Quack-Ups*
_____. *Chewy Chuckles*
_____. *Laughs on a Leash*
_____. *Monster Laughs*
Hall, Katy. *Batty Riddles*
_____. *Sheepish Riddles*
_____. *Turkey Riddles*

For Older Children

Dahl, Michael. *Roaring with Laughter*
_____. *Sit! Stay! Laugh!*
Fox, Lori Miller. *Riddle Riot*
Grambs, Alison. *Totally Silly Jokes*
Horsfall, Jacqueline. *Super Goofy Jokes*
Moore, Mark. *Beastly Laughs*
_____. *Creepy Crawlers*
Rosenberg, Pam. *School Jokes*
Rosenbloom, Joseph. *Biggest Riddle Book in the World*
Schultz, Sam. *Game-Day Gigglers*
Thomas, Lyn. *Ha! Ha! Ha!*
Ziegler, Mark. *Giggle Bubbles*
_____. *Goofballs*

Find **more** by looking for call number 818.54.

Your Library's Name

your street address
your city, state, zip
your phone number
your website address

Cool Things You Can Do with Your Quad-LINC Library Card

• Check out materials from ANY Quad-LINC library!
• Return Quad-LINC materials to ANY Quad-LINC library! (Return materials at the location that's most convenient for you.)
• Reserve Quad-LINC library materials from home! (Arrange to have them sent to the library where it's most convenient for you to pick them up.)
• Use computers in the library!

If you don't already have a free library card, apply for one soon at your hometown's library!

Bring two forms of ID that show your current address.

Use the Library at Home with Quad-LINC's Website! http://qls.rbls.lib.il.us

• Check your account!
  See what materials you have checked out.
  See when your materials are due.
  See if you have fines.
• Find out what materials libraries have!
• Renew your materials!
• Reserve books!

How to Reserve a Book on the Computer

• Click on the Place Hold button at the left.
• Enter bar code # on your library card.
• Enter last four digits of bar card # as PIN.
• Scroll down to the name of the library where you want to pick up books.
• Click on that library's name.
• Click on Place Hold.
• Click on OK.

The staff at the library you chose as the pickup site will contact you when your requests become available.
This is a *free* service!

From Dee Anderson, *Reading Is Funny!* (Chicago: ALA, 2009).

WHY SHOULD *YOU* GO TO THE LIBRARY?

Find out what awaits you at [your library's name].
Copy the underlined letters—in order—in the blanks below.

Why did the boxer go to the library?   to "hi<u>t</u> the books"

Why did the basketball player go to the library?   to <u>r</u>ead "tall tal<u>e</u>s"

Why did the elf go to the library?   to re<u>a</u>d "short stories"

Why did the skeleton go to the library?   to "bone up" for a te<u>st</u>

Why did the cat go to the library?   to chase the computer mo<u>u</u>se

Why did the cow go to the library?   to get "an-udde<u>r</u>" book

Why did Humpty Dumpty go to the library?   to borrow "yolk" (jok<u>e</u>) book<u>s</u>

Please visit [your library's name] soon and find

____ ____ ____ ____ ____ ____   ____ ____ ____ .

your street address
your city, state, zip
your phone number
your website address

From Dee Anderson, *Reading Is Funny!* (Chicago: ALA, 2009).

Sample handout for back of Why Should *You* Go to the Library? activity sheet

WHY SHOULD *YOU* GO TO THE LIBRARY?

To Borrow Our Treasures

We have *thousands* of books, magazines, recorded books,
books with recordings, CDs, DVDs, audiocassettes, videocassettes,
puppets, puzzles, and art reproductions.

[List all types of materials your library circulates.
Tell how to apply for a library card and supply information about loan
policies, e.g., the length of the circulation period, fines for overdue
materials, and renewal procedures.]

To Get Information

Reference librarians are always on duty to answer your questions.
This is a *free* service!

To Use Our Computers

Search the Internet, read your e-mail,
and play with educational software.

To Enjoy Our *Free* Programs

We regularly schedule story times and other
programs for children *and* adults.
[Include descriptions and times of specific programs.]

To Shop for Bargains

Browse our sale room to find used books and magazines at very low prices.

[Add reasons that fit your own library.]

[Dress up this flyer by superimposing a picture of an animal
or person mentioned in the riddles over a photograph of your library.]

From Dee Anderson, *Reading Is Funny!* (Chicago: ALA, 2009).

ANSWERS TO ACTIVITY SHEETS

Can You Fill in the Blanks?

1. g
2. d
3. f
4. a
5. h
6. e
7. c
8. b

Who Said That?

1. f
2. h
3. i
4. c
5. j
6. d
7. e
8. g
9. b
10. a

Who Wrote That?

1. j
2. d
3. g
4. a
5. h
6. c
7. i
8. b
9. e
10. f

Crack the Code!

1. "funny looks"
2. a "sports" car
3. a "gummy" bear
4. "Scooper-man"
5. catching "flies"
6. She "teased" it.
7. doors

SMILE! YOU CAN "BRUSH UP" ON TEETH AT YOUR LIBRARY

Taking Care of Your Teeth (617.6)

Katz, Bobbi—*Make Way for Tooth Decay*

Rowan, Kate—*I Know Why I Brush My Teeth*

Going to the Dentist (617.6)

Johnston, Marianne—*Let's Talk about Going to the Dentist*

Radabaugh, Melinda Beth—*Going to the Dentist*

Picture Book Stories (E)

Gomi, Taro—*The Crocodile and the Dentist*

Olson, Mary W.—*Nice Try, Tooth Fairy*

Steig, William—*Doctor De Soto*

Chapter Books (F)

Dadey, Debbie—*Hercules Doesn't Pull Teeth*

Greenburg, Dan—*Dr. Jekyll, Orthodontist*

Park, Barbara—*Junie B., First Grader: Toothless Wonder*

How to Find Others

Search the library's catalog for "dental care," "dentistry," "teeth," and "tooth fairy."

LAUGH WITH YOUR LIBRARY

Why are the teeth scared to go to the dentist?
> They're "yellow."

What do dentists put on hamburgers?
> "drill" pickles

Who collects the baby teeth that little weasels lose?
> the Tooth "Ferret"

Why do people talk more when they're cold than they do when they're hot?
> Their teeth "chatter."

Why do witches wear green eye shadow?
> It matches their teeth.

What do you call George Washington's false teeth?
> "presi-dentures"

What do you call dentures that cost a dollar?
> "buck" teeth

Why will the pie crust go to the dentist?
> to get a "filling"

You'll find more riddles at

YOUR LIBRARY'S NAME

> your street address
> your city, state, zip
> your phone number
> your website address

Visit Soon!

SMILE! YOUR LIBRARY HAS BOOKS ABOUT GOING TO THE DOCTOR

For Younger Children

Johnston, Marianne—*Let's Talk about Going to the Doctor*

Mattern, Joanne—*I Use Math at the Doctor's*

Radabaugh, Melinda Beth—*Going to the Doctor*

Rogers, Fred—*Going to the Doctor*

For Older Children

Brazelton, T. Berry—*Going to the Doctor*

Woods, Samuel—*The Pediatrician*

You'll find more books by looking at call numbers 610 and 618.92.

YOUR LIBRARY'S NAME

your street address
your city, state, zip
your phone number
your website address

Visit Soon!

LAUGH WITH YOUR LIBRARY

Why did the spider go to the doctor?
    It caught a "bug."

When are people rude to their doctors?
    when they stick out their tongues

Why did the silly kid call his doctor a thief?
    She "took" his temperature.

What did the doctor tell the patient who had a banana in each ear, a raisin in each eye, and a carrot sticking out of her nose?
    "You're not eating right."

What did the doctor say to the patient who felt like a pair of curtains?
    "Pull yourself together."

What did the doctor say to the patient who felt like a rubber band?
    "Snap out of it!"

Why did the doctor prescribe perfume for her patient with a stuffy nose?
    It made him smell better.

Why did the silly patient have trouble when the doctor told him to drink water thirty minutes before bedtime?
    He was full after drinking for five minutes.

**Find more riddles
in books
at your library!**

SMILE! YOUR LIBRARY HAS BOOKS ABOUT GETTING GLASSES

Picture Books

Brown, Marc—*Arthur's Eyes*

Brown, Marc—*Glasses for D.W.*

Willson, Sarah—*Hocus-Focus*

Chapter Books

Brinson, Cynthia—*Seeing Sugar*

Park, Barbara—*Junie B., First Grader (at Last!)*

Information Books

Dooley, Virginia—*I Need Glasses: My Visit to the Optometrist*

Shaughnessy, Diane—*Let's Talk about Needing Glasses*

Information about Eye Care

Curry, Don L.—*Take Care of Your Eyes*

Nelson, Robin—*Seeing and Hearing Well*

How to Find Others

Search the library's catalog for "eye juvenile literature" and "eyeglasses fiction."

Browse nonfiction sections for call numbers 611.84, 612.84, and 617.7.

LAUGH WITH YOUR LIBRARY

How did the eye doctor know her patient needed glasses before examining him?

He came in through the window.

Why did the leopard go to the eye doctor?

It kept seeing spots.

Why didn't the silly kid want to have her eyes checked?

She preferred them plain blue.

What will you get if you never clean your glasses?

"dirty looks"

What will your glasses become if you never clean them?

"specked-tacles"

What happened when the optician fell into the lens-grinding machine?

She made a "spectacle" of herself.

Where did the eye doctor build an office?

on a "site" for sore eyes

What do eye doctors like to eat?
"see-food" (seafood)

You'll find more riddles in books at

YOUR LIBRARY'S NAME

your street address
your city, state, zip
your phone number
your website address

Visit Soon!

SMILE! YOUR LIBRARY HAS BOOKS ABOUT PETS

Picture Books about Pets

Calhoun, Mary—Henry the Cat series

Galdone, Paul—*Puss in Boots*

Meddaugh, Susan—Martha series

Pilkey, Dav—*Dog Breath*

Pilkey, Dav—*Kat Kong*

Zion, Gene—*Harry the Dirty Dog*

Chapter Books about Pets

Alexander, Lloyd—*Time Cat*

Alexander, Lloyd—*Town Cats and Other Tales*

Birney, Betty—Humphrey series

Bunting, Eve—*The Summer of Riley*

Graeber, Charlotte—*Fudge*

Howe, James—Bunnicula series

King-Smith, Dick—*Harry's Mad*

Naylor, Phyllis Reynolds—Shiloh series

Swallow, Pamela Curtis—*Melvil and Dewey in the Fast Lane*

Vande Velde, Vivian—*Smart Dog*

Books about Pet Care

See books with call number 636.

LAUGH WITH YOUR LIBRARY

What do cats order at Dairy Queen?
"mice-cream" cones

Why do cats have whiskers?
Without hands, it's hard to shave.

What do you call robbers who steal cats?
"purr" snatchers

What's soft and furry and says "Beow"?
a cat with a cold

What happened when the dog went to the flea circus?
It "stole the show."

Why shouldn't you force napping puppies to tell the truth?
Let sleeping dogs "lie."

Why did the attack dog miss obedience school yesterday?
It took a "sic" (sick) day.

Why don't Dalmatians like to play hide-and-seek?
They're always "spotted."

Find many more riddles and stories at
YOUR LIBRARY'S NAME
your street address
your city, state, zip
your phone number
your website address

Visit Soon!

PICK A PUMPKIN BOOK AT YOUR LIBRARY

Books about Growing Pumpkins

Burckhardt, Ann—*Pumpkins*

Fridell, Ron—*The Life Cycle of a Pumpkin*

Gibbons, Gail—*The Pumpkin Book*

King, Elizabeth—*Pumpkin Patch*

Sloat, Teri—*Patty's Pumpkin Patch*

Titherington, Jeanne—*Pumpkin, Pumpkin*

Books about Buying Pumpkins

Hutchings, Amy—*Picking Apples and Pumpkins*

Rockwell, Anne—*Apples and Pumpkins*

Stories about Pumpkins

DeFelice, Cynthia—*Mule Eggs*

Dillon, Jana—*Jeb Scarecrow's Pumpkin Patch*

Gaines, Isabel—*Pooh's Pumpkin*

Herman, R. A.—*The Littlest Pumpkin*

Kroll, Steven—*The Biggest Pumpkin Ever*

Silverman, Erica—*Big Pumpkin*

How to Find Other Pumpkin Books

Search the library's catalog for "jack-o'-lanterns" and "pumpkins."

Browse nonfiction sections for call numbers 635.62, 641.3562, and 736.9.

Check our display of Halloween books.

LAUGH WITH YOUR LIBRARY

What would happen if a giant trampled your pumpkin patch?
　　You'd get "squash."

What can fix a broken jack-o'-lantern?
　　a pumpkin "patch"

What do you call chubby jack-o'-lanterns?
　　"plump-kins"

What do wild dogs in India carve on Halloween?
　　"jackal-lanterns"

Why do we carve pumpkins on Halloween?
　　Strawberries aren't in season.

Your Library's Name

your street address
your city, state, zip
your phone number
your website address

Visit Soon!

WHY WAS RIP VAN WINKLE SCARED OF GOING TO THE LIBRARY AFTER HIS TWENTY-YEAR NAP?

His books were way overdue!

DON'T GET CAUGHT NAPPING!

RENEW YOUR BOOKS AHEAD OF TIME.

RENEW BY PHONE.

Call [phone number].

Have your library card and materials next to the phone when you call.

RENEW BY COMPUTER.

Visit [your library's website].
See directions on the back.

RENEW IN PERSON.

Bring your library card and materials to the circulation desk.

HOW TO RENEW YOUR BOOKS BY COMPUTER

- Go to [your library's website].
- Click on My Account.
- Enter the bar code number on the back of your library card where it asks for Library Bar Code Number.
- Enter the last four digits of your bar code number where it asks for PIN.
- Click on Renew My Materials.
- If you want to renew everything, click on Renew All Items.
- If you want to renew only some of your materials, click in the circle in front of each item you are renewing. Then click on Renew Selected Items.
- The new due date will appear on the computer screen.

PLEASE NOTE: You can't renew materials you've renewed before or items with reserves on them.

FINES FOR OVERDUE MATERIALS

Books, magazines, recorded books, and CDs—10 cents per day

Videocassettes and DVDs— $1.00 per day

Your Library's Name
your street address
your city, state, zip
your phone number
your website address

WHEN ARE LIBRARY BOOKS LIKE PUPPIES?

when their pages are dog-eared

BOOKS ARE OUR TREASURES.
LET'S TREASURE OUR BOOKS.

Take good care of your library books.

Use this bookmark to keep your place.

Don't bend down the corners of pages.

Don't put books down with their pages open.

Make sure your hands are clean before you read.

Your Library's Name

your street address
your city, state, zip
your phone number
your website address

BOOKS ARE OUR TREASURES. LET'S TREASURE OUR BOOKS.

Why did the book have to go to the doctor?

Somebody hurt its "spine."

DON'T PUT BOOKS DOWN WITH THEIR PAGES OPEN.

What would you call Cynthia Rylant's dog books if someone read them with dirty hands?

Henry and "Smudge"

ALWAYS MAKE SURE YOUR HANDS ARE CLEAN BEFORE YOU READ.

What would you call Stan and Jan's books if someone spilled juice on them?

the "Beren-stained" Bears

KEEP BOOKS AWAY FROM FOOD, DRINKS, AND OTHER MESSY STUFF.

What should you do if your dog starts eating your library book?

Take the words right out of its mouth.

PUT BOOKS WHERE PETS CAN'T REACH THEM.

   From Dee Anderson, *Reading Is Funny!* (Chicago: ALA, 2009).

LAUGH WITH YOUR LIBRARY

Why do birds fly south for the winter?
  It's too far to walk.

Callie Anderson

What do you call Thomas Edison's
  electric lightbulb?
    a "bright idea"

Charlie Granet

What do dogs order at Dairy Queen?
  ice-cream "bones"

Willie Lynch

What happened when the rag doll
  made a movie?
    It "flopped."

Sophie Spurgetis

What's mean and green and picks on
  little tadpoles?
    a "bully-frog"

Molly Stahl

Where do butchers dance?
  the "meat ball"

Pearl Young

*Share These Laughs
with Friends!*

From Dee Anderson, *Reading Is Funny!* (Chicago: ALA, 2009).

SHARE THESE RIDDLES WITH FAMILY AND FRIENDS

Who writes nursery rhymes and makes many mistakes?

Mother "Goofs"

Who writes both nursery rhymes *and* scary stories?

Mother "Goose-bumps"

What would you get if you dropped your Mother Goose book in the mud?

nursery "grime"

What cow can jump higher than the moon?

They all can. The moon can't jump.

Why did the cow jump over the moon?

to get to the Milky Way

Why did Mother Goose have trouble eating?

Her dish ran away with her spoon.

SHARE THESE RIDDLES WITH FAMILY AND FRIENDS

Who writes nursery rhymes and makes many mistakes?

Mother "Goofs"

Who writes both nursery rhymes *and* scary stories?

Mother "Goose-bumps"

What would you get if you dropped your Mother Goose book in the mud?

nursery "grime"

What cow can jump higher than the moon?

They all can. The moon can't jump.

Why did the cow jump over the moon?

to get to the Milky Way

Why did Mother Goose have trouble eating?

Her dish ran away with her spoon.

SHARE THESE RIDDLES WITH FAMILY AND FRIENDS

Where do birds and squirrels go when they want to read books?

"branch" libraries

What do basketball players borrow from the library?

"tall tales"

What do elves borrow from the library?

"short stories"

What do rabbits borrow from the library?

"cotton-tales" (cottontails)

What do skunks borrow from the library?

best "smellers" (best sellers)

What do snakes borrow from the library?

"hiss-tory" books

What happened when the lion read a riddle book at the library?

It "roared" with laughter.

What did the early bird catch at the library?

the "book-worm"

You'll find more riddles in books at

Your Library's Name
your street address
your city, state, zip
your phone number
your website address

Please Visit Soon!

SHARE THESE RIDDLES WITH FAMILY AND FRIENDS

Where do birds and squirrels go when they want to read books?

"branch" libraries

What do basketball players borrow from the library?

"tall tales"

What do elves borrow from the library?

"short stories"

What do rabbits borrow from the library?

"cotton-tales" (cottontails)

What do skunks borrow from the library?

best "smellers" (best sellers)

What do snakes borrow from the library?

"hiss-tory" books

What happened when the lion read a riddle book at the library?

It "roared" with laughter.

What did the early bird catch at the library?

the "book-worm"

You'll find more riddles in books at

Your Library's Name
your street address
your city, state, zip
your phone number
your website address

Please Visit Soon!

SHARE THESE RIDDLES WITH FAMILY AND FRIENDS

What did one ghost say to the other ghost?

> "Do you believe in people?"

What's the first thing ghosts do when they get in a car?

> fasten their "sheet-belts"

What happened when the banana saw a ghost?

> The banana "split."

What happened when the potato saw a ghost?

> It jumped right out of its skin.

What do blackbirds become after seeing a ghost?

> "scared-crows"

What do kittens become after seeing a ghost?

> "scaredy-cats"

Why do people who've seen ghosts often become clowns?

> They're "scared silly."

What did the ghost win in the scaring contest?

> a "boo" ribbon

What happens when actors perform for ghosts?

> The audience "boos."

Why will reading ghost stories cool you off on hot summer days?

> They're "chilling."

SHARE THESE RIDDLES WITH FAMILY AND FRIENDS

What did one ghost say to the other ghost?

> "Do you believe in people?"

What's the first thing ghosts do when they get in a car?

> fasten their "sheet-belts"

What happened when the banana saw a ghost?

> The banana "split."

What happened when the potato saw a ghost?

> It jumped right out of its skin.

What do blackbirds become after seeing a ghost?

> "scared-crows"

What do kittens become after seeing a ghost?

> "scaredy-cats"

Why do people who've seen ghosts often become clowns?

> They're "scared silly."

What did the ghost win in the scaring contest?

> a "boo" ribbon

What happens when actors perform for ghosts?

> The audience "boos."

Why will reading ghost stories cool you off on hot summer days?

> They're "chilling."

SHARE THESE RIDDLES WITH FAMILY AND FRIENDS

What falls down in winter but never gets hurt?

    snow

What's white and cold and falls up?

    a mixed-up snowflake

Why did the silly kid wear only one boot?

    The snow was just one foot deep.

How do snowmen get information?

    They search the "Winter-net."

What do snowmen put in their coffee?

    "cold cream"

What do snowmen win at the Olympics?

    "cold" medals

Why is Frosty the Snowman popular?

    He's really "cool."

Where does Frosty go to dance?

    the "snow ball"

Where does Frosty keep his money?

    a "snow bank"

What does Frosty eat for breakfast?

    "snow flakes"

What does Frosty eat with spaghetti?

    snowballs

SHARE THESE RIDDLES WITH FAMILY AND FRIENDS

What falls down in winter but never gets hurt?

    snow

What's white and cold and falls up?

    a mixed-up snowflake

Why did the silly kid wear only one boot?

    The snow was just one foot deep.

How do snowmen get information?

    They search the "Winter-net."

What do snowmen put in their coffee?

    "cold cream"

What do snowmen win at the Olympics?

    "cold" medals

Why is Frosty the Snowman popular?

    He's really "cool."

Where does Frosty go to dance?

    the "snow ball"

Where does Frosty keep his money?

    a "snow bank"

What does Frosty eat for breakfast?

    "snow flakes"

What does Frosty eat with spaghetti?

    snowballs

Index

You may also be interested in

A Box Full of Tales: Including step-by-step instructions from concept through implementation and supplemented by programming tips, this resource includes detailed plans for fifty great story boxes with suggested books, fingerplays, songs, props, crafts, and sign language. From *ah-choo* to antlers, from monkey business to zoo escapes, this resource offers winning, stress-free library programs for children without the headaches and the hassles.

More Family Storytimes: This book from best-selling author Rob Reid features stories, fingerplays, songs, and movement activities to enhance the time families spend at the library. Brimming with all new material, *More Family Storytimes* offers practical, creative, and active storytime programs that will captivate audiences of all ages.

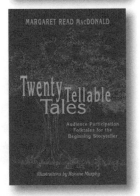

Twenty Tellable Tales: Filled with updated resources, classic stories from around the globe, guidelines to tell them with gusto, and advice on finding, learning, and telling new tales, this resource includes twenty stories, complete with suggestions for chants, songs, dialects, repeating lines, and audience participation that make these multicultural tales easy to learn and tell while satisfying young audiences.

Books in Bloom: Make great props in a reasonable amount of time with the thoroughly organized instructions, complete time lines, materials lists, and scripts provided in this must-have resource. For children's librarians, school media specialists, storytellers, teachers, and day-care workers who are willing to take the next step to transform storytime into a truly magical experience, this book will help spark the imaginations of those committed to sharing literature with children.

For more information on these and other great titles visit www.alastore.ala.org!

SEP   2009

CLIFTON PARK-HALFMOON PUBLIC LIBRARY, NY

0 00 06 0343454 9